LATE EXTRA!
Hackney in the News

DAVID MANDER

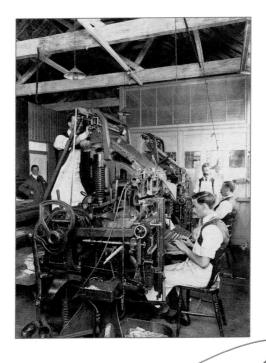

LONDON BOROUGH OF HACKNEY
SUTTON PUBLISHING LIMITED

Sutton Publishing Limited
Phoenix Mill · Thrupp · Stroud
Gloucestershire · GL5 2BU
in association with
Hackney Archives Department

First published 2000

Copyright © David Mander, 2000

Title page photograph: The linotype press of
the *Hackney Gazette*, *c*. 1925.

British Library Cataloguing in Publication Data
A catalogue record for this book is available from the
British Library.

ISBN 0-7509-2528-0

Typeset in 10.5/13.5 Photina.
Typesetting and origination by
Sutton Publishing Limited.
Printed and bound in England by
J.H. Haynes & Co. Ltd, Sparkford.

ACKNOWLEDGEMENTS

Thanks are due to the Editor and proprietors of the *Hackney Gazette* for permission to reprint pieces from the paper and those of its predecessors taken over from the former owners, Potters Press. Thanks to the *Gazette* also for allowing the pictures from past copies of the paper to be reproduced from Hackney Archives Department's cuttings books or from the original newspapers. Sadly, the original photographs and negatives taken before 1983 in the main have not survived and only the view on the title page comes from an original print. Other views taken from the *Hackney Gazette* are: pp. 1, 2, 3, 5, 32 (top), 34, 42, 44, 51, 52, 63, 64, 65, 66, 76, 90, 96, 101, 102, 103, 104, 106, 110, 115, 119 and 121. Additional thanks to Mrs E. Whitby for the photograph on p. 94. Other pictures are from the visual collections and library series scrapbooks held at Hackney Archives Department.

Some of the pieces in Chapter One, the Monkey Parade', the Hackney Carnival and the death of Queen Victoria in Chapter Three, the 1888 school piece in Chapter Five, the Hackney Downs section in Chapter Six and the escaped bull story in Chapter Nine made their first appearance as part of *Hackney Voices*, an entertainment of prose and music originally performed for the Friends of Hackney Archives. My thanks to my original fellow editor and reader Isobel Watson and to my fellow readers Jenny Golden and the late Martin Bidmead. Parts of the introduction also appeared in the *Hackney Gazette* 130th anniversary issue of 1994. Choosing copy for *Late Extra!* was a difficult task with limitations of space and there were many pieces that clamoured for admission, while to have covered in full a major topic like housing would have taken up the entire book. I have attempted to provide a mixture of serious source material and lighter pieces, and if the content amuses or provokes thought – or better still encourages the reader to come and use the local papers held at Hackney Archives Department and the British Library – then so much the better. A leaflet is available from Hackney Archives Department which details the newspapers and magazines held there; restrictions on space have prevented inclusion of this information here. Reader and author both owe a final debt of gratitude to the journalists and, latterly, newspaper photographers who hammered out the deathless prose, got the pose and made the copy deadline.

David Mander
September 2000

CONTENTS

Feathers and confetti in the East End: a coster's wedding at Shoreditch.

Daily Graphic, 11 May 1905: MAY WEDDING IN SHOREDITCH

There has been a block of traffic several mornings this week in Shoreditch, just where the trams from the Hackney Road meet the traffic of the Shoreditch High Street and the vans from Old Street. But no-one seemed to take it amiss; the omnibus drivers grinned cheerfully at one another, and nodded towards Shoreditch Church with a wink, towards which every passenger on the omnibuses turned an interested eye. About the railings clustered the pick of the neighbourhood; ladies from the model dwellings round about Columbia Market, who had forgotten to arrange their hair, but who had considerately brought their babies to attend the ceremony; the odd job men from the public-houses about the Haggerston Road; and a few stragglers from Hoxton. At one end of the social scale were the friends of the bridegroom, who had been too wary to go into the church, but who were conspicuous by reason of an unusual cleanliness of collar or a dazzling brightness of cravat; and at the other end were the youth of the neighbourhood, in the remnants of their father's trousers or the fragments of their mother's boots. It was freely rumoured on the omnibuses . . . that this was the seventh wedding that had taken place this morning . . . But everyone was too excited for conversation, there was an uneasy feeling that the block might break up and the commanding arm of the policeman bid us move on before we saw the bride . . . the eye of the Force was itself furtively gliding towards the church door. Suddenly it opened . . . it was the bride herself; a cheery young woman with an ostrich feather that would have challenged a comet for brightness. . . . It was a great moment for [the bridegroom] but he was hardly conscious of it, being . . . principally occupied in dodging showers of rice and an acclamatory boot. When Shoreditch does throw rice (or old boots), it does the thing thoroughly . . . for a moment the bride and bridegroom stood fire, then dropping arms and linking hands, they fled – raced towards the gates; and in a moment, as it were, were lost in the crowd, who laughed and cheered and slapped them on the back. . . .

CHAPTER ONE

INTRODUCTION

The printing presses in Richmond Road have rolled off the last of the 20,000 print run of the *Hackney Gazette* and the papers, already folded and counted into dozens, are being bundled out of the doors and on to the waiting box tricycles. Last-minute directions are given, and then the third issue of the week is peddled off at top speed to newsagents across Hackney, Stoke Newington, Bethnal Green, Shoreditch, Islington and Tottenham. A small crowd waiting outside the print works have already secured their own copies – for this was the world of the early 1920s where the local papers between them had a monopoly on the latest events in the area, and for many people were the source of news and views on national events as well.

The *Hackney Gazette* was not the first locally produced newspaper, nor was it the first attempt by printer Charles Potter, whose two previous papers had not lasted. Making sure of his market, Potter plastered Hackney with handbills in April 1864, announcing the birth of 'a free liberal and patriotic journal, especially devoted to the interests of ratepayers' which aimed to provide 'full and faithful reports of all parochial, political, religious and other meetings, together with all incidents of public interest, correspondence, historical

Crowds outside the printing office of the *Hackney Gazette*.

reminiscences' and which would appear weekly. Advertisers were assured that they would be given a new and hitherto unattainable channel.

Initially reporters were all volunteers from the Reform Party, which the *Gazette* naturally supported, indeed these journalists on occasions chaired the meetings they covered! Early editorials were written by Aaron Ayshford, and the day-to-day affairs were run by John Henry Bowack, manager of the printing department. The early volunteers soon found that the burden of producing a paper to time conflicted with other duties and salaried staff took over. The first paid editor seems to have been William Phillips, formerly a Customs and Excise man and known to his friends as

Delivery bikes at the ready outside the *Hackney Gazette* offices, Kingsland Road.

'The Captain'. With his large balding head and long Edward Lear-like beard, The Captain must have been a considerable presence in the editor's chair. He also wrote a column called Our Local Flaneur (one who strolls about, idles and observes) on current topics. His interests included bibliography, antiquities and music, and he led the choir at St Phillip's Church, Dalston. His successor, Henry Browne, was an ardent teetotaller and never missed an opportunity to promote the temperance cause in his columns.

Initially the *Gazette* appeared on Saturdays only, in the standard broadsheet format with adverts taking up the front page. In the early years it ran to just four pages, with the first also listing coming events ranging from the new programmes at the Shoreditch theatres through to lectures and even the launch of dancing classes at Stoke Newington College. Page two carried the editorial, which appeared under a little sketch of the Old Church Tower, ancestor of the modern *Gazette* logo. On to the same page were squeezed marriage and death announcements and reports of meetings of local clubs and societies. Page three carried reports of the meetings of local government bodies and correspondence, together with the text of the most notable sermon of the week. Illustrations were confined to one or two small line drawings in the adverts. Illustrations

Charles Potter, printer and newspaper publisher in Hackney in the nineteenth century.

proper were many years away but towards the end of the nineteenth century pictures of products on sale became ever bolder. For some reason purveyors of dentures led the way, featuring the product under the bold heading 'TEETH! TEETH! TEETH!' just in case the casual reader had missed the point. Sports reporting was strictly confined to the activities of local clubs and teams.

The *Hackney Gazette* was not first in the field and had a number of competitors over the years. Rivals included the *Shoreditch Observer & Hackney Express* (1857–1915), founded as 'a municipal journal for the Eastern, Central and North Eastern districts' and as 'a journal of political and social progress, advancing parliamentary reform [the extension of the rights to vote], vote by ballot, short parliaments and equal electoral districts, economies in government and administration reform in every department

The billboard advertising the first issue of the *Hackney Gazette* in 1864.

Seeing in the new century – 'Ye Venerable St John-of-Hackney pondereth well the Question of Parish Boundaries.' A cartoon from the *Hackney Mercury*, 6 January 1900, drawing inspiration from the boundary changes brought in with the formation of the new metropolitan boroughs.

of the public service', which should have been enough to keep the bulk of its readership happy. Other papers included the *Eastern Post* (1868–1938, originally based in Shoreditch) and the *Hackney Mercury* (1885–1910), in whose pages local doctor Benjamin Clarke contributed his memories of Hackney of the 1830s and 1840s. The *Mercury* was firmly in favour of the connection between Church and State and supported the Conservatives, providing large portraits and biographies of candidates and publishing criticism of local and national Liberals – Gladstone naturally came in for a bad time in early editions. There were also papers based in Stoke Newington, including the *North London Guardian* (1888–1916) produced almost singlehanded by local teacher and antiquarian

J.R. Spratling until its demise during the First World War, reputedly for running foul of the censor.

It was not just the *North London Guardian* that had the minimum of paid staff. Many of the local papers had few employees. Issues of the *Shoreditch Observer* ran to just four pages in 1880, and principally covered local government reports with a few literary pieces and general articles as well as the inevitable crime and inquest stories. The *Hackney Gazette*'s David Duncan claimed never to have met an editor of the *Hackney Mercury*, his only contact being a lone journalist who 'latterly appeared to be obsessed with a secret sorrow'.

Relatively few local papers published more than weekly, though the *Hackney Spectator*, founded in 1901 and with a lively ear for scandal, came out on Mondays and Fridays. With a large and young staff, Duncan recalled that they so crowded the public gallery at Hackney Town Hall that the Council set a limit of not more than two reporters per paper. Weekly papers like the *Hackney & Stoke Newington Recorder* ran to eight pages in the 1920s and carried sections on gardening, literary articles, poultry rearing, pieces for women and local entertainment – which on 6 January 1928 included the visit of the latest group from the USA, W.H. Garland's 'Brown Birds' and the Charleston Syncopation Orchestra. There were even brief weather forecasts from 1923, something earlier papers seemed to have neglected. The serialization of stories also helped sell papers – in 1904 the *Hackney Express* carried one by Arthur Conan Doyle.

The coverage of entertainment varied. The *Hackney Mercury* and the *Eastern Post* both carried reviews of local productions – in the nineteenth century it was the Shoreditch theatres, in the twentieth the Hackney Empire and the Dalston Theatre. In the Victorian period the local paper was also the source for national news and as late as 1914 the *North London Guardian* was informing its readers of the problems the islanders of the Grand Cayman were experiencing with crabs and, perhaps with greater relevance, warning of the dumping of cheap eggs imported from Riga (now in Latvia). While there was reasonable coverage of inquests, announcements of births, deaths and marriages are unusual, though the *Hackney Gazette* did give a selection in some issues from the 1870s onwards. Obituary pieces only went in if the person was or had been a local worthy – a clergyman, or businessman or significant local politician.

Changes in production methods allowed papers to grow in size and expand in content after the First World War. Photographic reproduction was used sparingly from the 1920s, but was only really commonplace after the Second World War. Sadly the majority of the *Hackney Gazette* photographs taken before 1983 do not survive in the original and nothing has been preserved of the local commercial press except the papers themselves.

The *Hackney Gazette* is the only local paper still in existence in Hackney, having taken over some of its rivals. From its initial Saturday issue, the *Gazette* added a Wednesday paper in 1871 to keep pace with expanding advertising, moving to a Friday from Saturday before 1875. In November of that year the *Gazette* increased its print run again to three issues a week, with the appearance of a Monday paper. Adverts filled the back and front of the papers for the next sixty-four years and it took the trauma of the outbreak of the Second World War to produce the modern front page, ousting the all important business of selling motor cars to page two.

One cub reporter who joined the *Gazette* aged twenty in 1897 was to make his mark. Prophetically the proprietor of the time, Charles Potter, wrote in his letter appointing Duncan, 'In we suit one another, there is no reason why you should not remain with us for years'. David Duncan did just that, becoming editor in 1911 and remaining in post until his retirement in 1949. Duncan also wrote a weekly column as well as leading articles and had a wide range of contacts. He had originally intended to try to be neutral in his coverage, but rapidly concluded that a strong stance made for a better paper. He was also knowledgable on local history and used this to good effect in the sixtieth anniversary commemorative booklet published by the newspaper in 1924.

David Duncan, editor of the *Hackney Gazette* from 1911 to 1949.

In 1911 the *Gazette* was printed on a flat-bed machine – one sheet at a time – and had a circulation of about 4,000. It was supposed to be the longest paper in London and dropped or flopped on library desks. Rotary and Linotype presses speeded up production, and circulation of what were then three weekly issues stood at 130,000 in 1949. Distribution also improved – the pony cart of early days was replaced by a fleet of box tricycles and later motor vans.

What did the *Gazette* choose to report in its early years? The newspaper was launched on a Hackney in the throes of building development and railway speculation. Tollgates on main roads had only just been abolished and many new roads were not properly made and turned into smelly muddy tracks in wet weather. Old houses and estates were giving way to new streets and inhabitants and industry was gaining a wider foothold. There were still farms and the commons were used for grazing but the battle over those who wanted to use them for recreation with farmers and gravel extractors was about to be joined. The *Gazette* took a stand on some of the railway schemes and claimed to have played its part in ensuring that the Great Eastern Railway tunnelled under Hackney Downs, rather than put the route through an open cutting as the company originally wished. It is a pity that there was not a similar campaign to save Stoke Newington Common, but the early twenty-first-century reader, armed with the knowledge of what actually happened, is likely to be surprised at what did not make the pages of the *Gazette* – the opening of the horse tramway along Mare Street for instance.

As for what came later, this book attempts to provide a small selection. With so much material to chose from it is difficult to be fully representative. Prose styles were more verbose in the past, which has led to a degree of editing and in some cases summaries of reports are given rather than the full original. Some stories required rather more background than space allowed and time precluded going through every year and so some periods are better represented than others. I have chosen to end the selection in the early 1980s, as I am not sure that sufficient perspective exists on more modern pieces. For the period before the advent of local newspapers I have drawn on the extensive cuttings collections held at Hackney Archives Department and have tried to provide a mixture of the historically useful and the plain entertaining. As in other areas of the book, the selection on crime considerably under-represents the amount of reporting – but as a former neighbour of mine in Hackney commented, 'We never buy the *Gazette* – there is too much crime in it!'

The *Hackney Gazette* remained in the hands of the Potter family until the mid-1980s and now forms part of the Independent Newspaper (U.K.) group. Originally based at 440 Kingsland Road, with a printing works on the corner of Richmond and Glebe roads, it moved to 505a Kingsland Road in 1924, to 250–6 Kingsland Road in 1958 and is now based in Cambridge Heath Road. It was still producing two issues up to the mid-1980s, when the Tuesday issue was replaced by a free paper, the *Hackney Echo*, which ceased in 1999. When Hackney became the supposed setting for the BBC's *EastEnders*, the paper also stood in for the programme's 'Walford Gazette'. Headlines and prose style have emulated the tabloids and full-colour front pages appeared in the mid-1990s.

Since its inception in 1965, Hackney Archives Department has served as the repository for the *Hackney Gazette* and holds the majority of past local newspapers, either in the original or as microfilm copies of originals that are held at the British Library Newspaper Library in Colindale in North London. The Archives Department has also produced a leaflet listing the titles it holds, with covering dates. Hackney Archives Department is one of many libraries and record offices in the London and South Eastern Library Region of England to take part in a regional plan to preserve local newspapers. At a national level, this Newsplan programme has just received Heritage Lottery funding to help with the filming of the scarce and the fragile – for it is still impossible to restore original newspapers, printed on poor-quality paper and designed to be thrown away. Microfilm reduces wear and tear on the originals and helps ensure that family historians, businesses, community groups, schools and the simply curious can continue to use this fascinating record of the distant past – and more recent times and events.

CHAPTER TWO

BEFORE THE LOCAL PAPERS, 1720–1857

This selection of cuttings taken from national and regional papers has been grouped into themes.

CRIME AND ACCIDENTS

1722

A few days ago two Lads had some Words at Mr W——'s Boarding School in Hackney: the one being stronger than the other ty'd him up by his Hands to a Beam in his Room, and after having stript and beat him, he Drew his Sword and stabbed him in several Places under the Arm; which not content with, the cruel Youth exercised his Penknife on him too. He then took him down, and finding he was not despatch'd, hung him up again by the neck, and so left him; but some other Lad coming into the Room just afterwards, took him down, and he is now in a fair way of Recovery. Let this Caution all parents how they arm their Children with Swords, before they have Discretion enough to rule their Passions.

13 September 1729

Last week a Coach going to Hackney, in which were Four Gentlemen, was attack'd by a Highwayman, who demanded their Money, which they not caring to part with, looked out of the Coach, and seeing at some Distance a person on Horseback, called out to him for Assistance, who made what Haste he could; which the Highwayman seeing, rode off; but on the Person's coming up to the Coach, and enquiring what was the Matter, they immediately pursued him, and being well mounted, overtook him in a Lane leading to a Farm House, where the Highwayman being at a Stand (it being no Road Way) fired at the Person who pursu'd him, but missing him was presently taken, by the Assistance of several who came on hearing the Report of the Pistol, and being carried before a Magistrate, proves to be a Weaver in Spittlefields.

1750

One Charles Isaacs, at Hackney, being bit by a mad Dog about six Months ago, died one day this Week raving mad:- a shocking Calamity, and it were much to be wished that the great Number of unhappy Persons who are thus destroyed may alarm the Legislature so as to oblige People not to keep any other Dogs, but such as are really useful.

14 April 1752

The Thieves in and about Hackney have begun to rob the hen-houses, and steal the Poultry thereabouts. Mr Ram of Homerton lost his Stock of Fowls about a Week ago; Mr Albert also lost Part of his Stock about the same Time. Its is suprizing that Gentlemen have not the Spirit to exert themselves in the Discovery and Punishment of a Class of Scoundrels, whose Rogueries are the more provoking, as the Mischief they do (however it may effect the Losers) produces them so little. The finest Fowls these Villians take, being too old and lean for the Spit; yet they must kill them, in order to carry them off without Noise. Tis said the poor People commonly buy dead Fowls in Spital-Fields Market, early in a Morning, with the Feathers on, for about six Pence a Piece. What despicable Villains must these be, who will venture the Penalty of the laws for so wretched a Consideration!

March 1763

Tuesday afternoon as a lady was returning in her chariot to Walthamstow, in the new road leading over Hackney Marsh a party of sailors surrounded the chariot. The Lady, being greatly terrified, offered them her purse, which the honest Tars refused, saying 'Madam, we want no money, only "tip us your daddle"'; the meaning of which expression being explained, they had all the honour of shaking hands with her and went away highly satisfied.

December 1772

It is observable that for many weeks past there has not been a single Robbery on the Hackney road, owing to the excellent Disposition of the Lamps, and the Number and Vigilance of the Watchmen.

1777, REWARDS

The Inhabitants of Hackney, taking into Consideration the great Increase of Robberies in the Parish; and many daring Attempts to break into the Houses of the Inhabitants, do hereby give Notice, that they have by private Subscription raised a Fund for Payment of the following Rewards for apprehending any Person or Persons who shall commit any of the following Offences in the Said Parish.

For every Offender who shall commit a Burglary or Robbery in any Dwelling House in the Night, £40, to wit £10 on Commitment for the Offence and £30 on Conviction, over and above the public Reward of £15 already offered by the Parish. . . .

For every Highwayman or Footpad £20 [£5 on commitment, £15 on conviction]

For every Offender who shall commit any Felony or Robbery in any Outhouse, Barn, stable, Garden, Orchard or Fishpond or shall steal any Poultry, Iron Rails or Lead, from any Dwelling-House, or Building, £10 [£3 on commitment, £7 on conviction]

For every Offender who shall steal any Horse, Mare or Gelding, Ox, Cow or Heifer, £10. . . .

For every Offender who shall steal any Calf, Sheep or Hog, £2 on Conviction.

For every Offender who shall unlawfully and maliciously kill, maim, would or disfigure any Cattle £2 on Conviction

For every Offender who shall steal or destroy any Tree, Shrub, Plant, or any Kind of Paling or fence, to the amount of Five Shillings, £2 on Conviction. . . .

However, penalties were not enough to stop robberies. In August 1782 one gang went on a spree that started in a house near Well Street, where they broke into the nursery by mistake and in frustration set fire to the house. The robbers then went on up Mare Street to what is now Clarence Road, breaking into three other houses, and although driven off by the barking of a dog from one house, were able to get away without being challenged.

1783

Yesterday morning about three o-clock, a young man genteelly dressed was taken in Hackney Park, stealing a deer; and when taken before a magistrate, it is remarkable that, in preference to a year's imprisonment, he voluntarily offered to stand in the pillory this day about four o'clock, for one hour, in the Park adjoining Homerton; there were found on him at the time he was taken, 22 guineas and a cutlass.

27 June 1783

Early this morning a black servant belonging to a gentleman near Kingsland met two of the patrole on the Kingsland-road, and mistaking them for suspected persons rashly fired a blunderbus, which severely wounded one of the patrole. The black was immediately pursued and the same day committed to Clerkenwell-prison.

London Magazine, 17 May 1787

A remarkable instance of the hand of Providential justice was exhibited last Monday at Hoxton. On the Saturday previous to that day, a man took the diabolical resolution of destroying his wife and children; to perpetrate which, he bought a leg of mutton, and rubbed it over with a considerable quantity of arsenic; so done, he took it home, and told his wife to dress the mutton on Sunday, and as he did not expect to be at home, he desired that she and the children might eat it, without waiting for him. On Sunday the mutton was dressed, but he not coming home, his wife, not wishing to eat it without his being at dinner, made some yeast dumplings for herself and children, and left the mutton uneaten. He did not return that evening, and still the leg of mutton remained whole; but on Monday he came home and brought with him a few flat fish (as supposed to save the appearance of guilt, expecting his family to have been poisoned). On seeing his wife, he, somewhat agitated, asked her, if she and the children were in health, and being answered that they were well, he asked whether they had eaten the mutton? The wife told him it had been dressed, but he not coming home they had made their dinner on dumplings and the mutton they had not touched. At that answer he appeared much vexed and surlily ordered his wife to dress him some of the flat fish. She immediately dressed him three, and he sat down and eat [*sic*] them. Directly afterwards, in great confusion, he asked his wife in what she had fried the fish, and on being told the dripping from the mutton which had been dressed on Sunday, he exclaimed 'Then I am a dead man.' He then made a full confession of his wicked intention, and in two hours afterwards, expired in great agonies.

3 July 1801

Morality was at issue when a magistrate at Worship Street court was faced with a case arising from the Lascar (usually Indian) seamen, employed by the East India Company. A complaint was made by a Hackney Road resident, behind whose house the Company had built one of its set of barracks for the seamen while their ships were in port in London (the other was in Kingsland Road). He stated:

. . . that, owing to the irregular conduct of these men, the neighbourhood had been much disturbed, and that this irregularity had arisen from their connection with a number of idle and dissolute girls, who notwithstanding the vigilance of the porter at the door, find means to gain admission to them. Four of these girls were brought into custody, who were taken into the barracks, in which there are now more than forty men. The eldest of these girls was only twenty; two of them had not attained their sixteenth year. They came from Cable-street and had been at the barracks the whole of the night. It appeared by their connection with girls of this description, many of the men had become diseased, and that some had died in consequence. Several of the Lascars attended, and wished, with great gallantry, to release their paramours, but the Magistrate considered this case as of so serious a nature, that he committed them as idle disorderly, and persons of ill fame.

The solution, the magistrate suggested, was to build barracks on the coast, where he thought the problem of attendant prostitutes would be avoided as would 'the insults to which these people are liable arising from brickmakers etc'.

31 August 1801

On Friday last the lock was stolen off the door of Hackney church, during the time of divine service! This is the most impudent robbery that has been committed for some time.

9 October 1819

The voluntary examination of John Homesby, bricklayer's labourer taken by . . . justices . . . for the Cinque Ports [for the murder of his wife Ann Homesby, aged twenty, found murdered, by wounds with an axe, in her father's cottage, opposite the Crooked Billet on 28 September 1819].

According to another report, Homesby, born in Hackney, had gone to sea, and returning some four years before, had met up with and married Ann. It was claimed that disagreements arose once his money was exhausted, since he was described as 'profligate' and unable to keep her. She applied for parish relief, but was told she was young and able to work; she afterwards became loose in her manners and they separated. The husband went to work with bricklayers, but still he sought her and occasionally they met upon friendly terms. Her father gave them every encouragement in his power, but all would not appease them.

John Homesby confessed to the murder of his wife . . . having on Tuesday evening week, about . . . dusk . . . caught her in the act of adultery, in a cow hovel, opposite her father's house at Clapton – [he] accompanied his wife home to her father's house; he was gone on his watch, when they got home; he then told the housekeeper, . . . [Esther] Surrey, of the adultery of his wife, and . . . directly after, his wife and him had an altercation about going to bed together; and he, having struck her slightly with his open hand, she threatened if he did not come to bed to her, she would . . . go to those she had left, and, as he had struck her, she would swear her life against him, and he should lay in gaol and rot; and she would go and live with the other man [Lawrence], whom she loved. After this he walked out and in the room two or three times and she declared on his hesitating to come to bed with her, with violent oaths, that she would be the death of one or the other of them. He then went for an axe that lay in the adjoining room, close by her father's chest; and . . . challenged her to say so again. She said, rather than suffer the usage she had, she would be the death of one or the other. At this instance, he struck her upon the head with the back of the axe, slightly. She was then sitting on the bed, partly undressed, having previously seemed to attempt to dress herself again. When she said she would go to the other man, after the first blow was struck, he had just time to hear her say 'Oh! You know;' and a second blow with the back of the axe immediately followed. He does not know whether he struck her more or not. She seemed to swoon on the right side and bled . . . He then took her in by the left arm, and pulling her to the left side of the bed, kissed her, saying 'my dear, you was once my comfort for a little time; and now I am the death of you and you of me.' She was then alive and was so when he left the room, and went to her father's chest, and took a pound note out of it and escaped – having threatened to the children and the housekeeper he would be the death of them, if they made any noise. . . . He came to Woolwich about nine or ten o'clock the next morning – and was at Canterbury last Sunday – was at Dover yesterday – and has wandered about at different places without any particular intention, til he came to Walmer. He wishes to add, that on his wife's making an excuse that she had been dragged into the cow-house by great force, by the man he found her with, he . . . offered, if she would swear the rape against him, she should be forgiven; but she refused in coarse language, saying 'She loved his little finger better than her husband's whole body.'.

Homesby was tried at the Old Bailey on 28 October 1819, found guilty by the jury and sentenced to death on the following Monday, with his body to go for dissection. Homesby went to the scaffold protesting his love for his former wife and sang a hymn before his hanging.

SPORT AND DIVERSIONS

29 April 1751

On Saturday the young Gentlemen educated at Mr Newcomb's School at Hackney, performed one of Terence's Plays, in which the young Earl of Euston play'd a part; his Grace the Duke of Grafton, his Lordship's Grandfather, honoured the Performance with his Presence.

Newcomb's Hackney School viewed from the rear, *c.* 1820.

1765

To be seen at Mr Cotton's, in Coopers Gardens, Hackney Road, at sixpence each person, a surprising white Dutch radish, measures two Feet two Inches round; it is allowed by all the Gardeners to be the greatest Curiousity that was ever seen.

c. 1788

An uncommon method of inhuman sport and which is to be celebrated weekly during the winter, was exhibited on Wednesday afternoon near the Shoulder of Mutton and Cat. In Sun Tavern Fields, viz a pig clean shaved, and soaped upon the tail, was turned out to be caught by any person, who holding it by the tail and throwing it over his head, was entitled to a gold laced hat, which was elevated upon a pole. Many attempts were made, but none of them were effectual within the time of running, owing to the competitors pulling each other down etc. However the shrieking of the animal, and the hallooing of the company, caused much diversion, to the disgrace of the brutes concerned.

7 July 1790, BOXING

Sunday morning, at five o'clock, a battle was fought in a field near Homerton, between *Long Larry*, the noted Dog-seller about Hackney, and *Timothy Power*, a Coal-heaver, well known about Wapping by the appellation of *Bryan O'Linn*.

The quarrel originated in a political discussion at a public house in Covent Garden, last Friday, when it was agreed mutually, to decide it in a private way, and to allow none but friends to be present, among whom *Bryan O'Linn*'s wife actually officiated as his bottle-holder.

From the secrecy with which the whole was conducted, the Greys did not make their appearance; and the betting Amateurs were all excluded from the sight of a battle, which was as desperate as it was singular, from the mode in which it was managed; for *Fanny the black fish-woman* was bottle-holder to *Long Larry*.

The Cat and Mutton, London Fields. Watercolour by C. Bigot.

The battle lasted forty-three minutes, during which each party received and returned several severe blows. *Bryan O'Linn* had his cheek laid open, and lost three of his teeth; and his antagonist had one of his ears almost torn off. At length *Long Larry*, attempting to guard a feint blow aimed at his right side, received so dreadful a blow in his left eye, that it was struck out of his head in a most shocking manner, when he immediately gave in; but *Bryan O'Linn*, notwithstanding his victory, received such a bruising that it is imagined he cannot survive it.

29 July 1791, BULL BAITING AT HACKNEY [*An article produced in support of the lack of police near London.*]

Friday afternoon a Bull was baited near Temple Mills, upon Hackney Marshes; [watched by upwards of three thousand people who] had assembled by four o'clock. The bull was brought to the stake soon after that hour; and after twelve dogs had run at him, he broke loose. A strange scene of uproar and confusion ensued, hackney coaches and jockey carts ran in every direction, horsemen riding against each other, many hundreds of people tumbling one upon another, and the rest running different ways to avoid the fury of the enraged animal, which tossed a girl of about nine years old, who fortunately, however, received no material hurt.

A view across Hackney Marshes near the White Bridge. Watercolour by Walter Fisher, 1868.

The bull was again brought to the stake, and worried by eight more dogs, one of which attacked him at a time. The bull being taken away, two men, a chimney sweep, and a butcher, came into the ring to fight for four guineas: they maintained a severe contest for near three quarters of an hour, when a dispute arising about the fairness of a blow, they retired each into a hackney coach.

The bull was now a third time brought to the stake, and after being again baited, was led from the ring, which was immediately after entered by the chimney sweep and the butcher, who fought obstinately for half an hour, when victory was declared for the former. The bull being again brought to the stake, was baited till the approach of evening, when he was wickedly let loose among the crowd, which by this time had greatly increased, by a concourse of people of all descriptions, not only from London, but the adjacent villages. While at liberty, the bull tossed an elderly man, but he received no injury.

During the tumult and uproar of the afternoon, a vast number of people had their pockets picked, or were otherwise robbed of their watches, money etc. A young man, servant to a brazier at Stratford, having informed a gentleman that he had just seen a fellow pick his pocket, the poor man was instantly surrounded by a gang of villains, who beat him in a most barbarous way and, in all probability, would have murdered him, had they not been interrupted, in the exercise of their brutal fury, by the bull being let loose; which circumstance afforded their victim an opportunity of getting to the side of the Lead Mill River, where he was received into a boat and conveyed to the opposite shore.

28 August 1836, MORE BALLOON FOOLERY

The balloon ascent made by Mrs Graham from the Mermaid Gardens, 1837.

Tuesday evening from the gardens of the Mermaid Tavern, Hackney for the benefit of the widow of the late Mr Cocking. Attached to the balloon were two parachutes, models of those used by M. Garnerin and Mr Cocking, the descent of which was intended to show the comparative safety of their particular structure. The parachutes were of cotton and the framework of cane. In an apartment of the tavern were exhibited the model of Mr Cocking's parachute, manu-factured by himself, and in one corner of the room were the remains of the parachute with which Mr Cocking made his fatal experiment. At about quarter past six, the inflation of the balloon being completed, a bar of wood was placed across the car, along the upper surface of which ran a cord passing through holes at each extremity. To the ends of the cord were attached the respective parachutes, so that by cutting the cord in the centre they would descend at the same moment. Mrs Graham entered the car, accompanied by a Mr John Adams, and the balloon ascended. At an altitude of 600 or 700 feet, Mrs Graham cut the cord and the parachutes descended. Some seconds elapsed before the model of M. Garnerin's parachute opened, and when it did the oscillation complained of on the occasion of the actual descents of that gentleman took place; that of Mr Cocking was somewhat slower in its descent and very steady. The parachutes fell in the grounds of a gentleman near the place of ascent and were shortly afterwards brought back to the gardens.

TRAVEL

22 December 1769, To all Hackney Coachmen

The Trustees of the Hackney Turnpike Road, having taken into Consideration the many Complaints which have been made of accidents and Inconveniences arising from the standing of Coaches in the narrow Part of Church-street in Hackney, between the Brook and Ward's Corner, to prevent the same in future, give Notice to all Hackney Coachmen, that Boards are put up within the above Distance, directing them where they may place their Coaches; and if any Coachman shall place his Coach on any other part of the Road there, he will be prosecuted by the Trustees.

NB the Trustees have provided Places for seven Coaches to stand within the above Distance, and also at a great Expense a proper and convenient Place for thirteen coaches more on the cross Road leading from the Blue Post to the Five Houses.

28 April 1848, To the Editor of *The Times*

Sir,
On Good Friday morning last my son and daughter were going to church, when suddenly they found the earth give way under their feet in the middle of the public pathway. My son was fast disappearing and my daughter also, but by violent struggling they were both miraculously preserved.

In the centre of Mare-street, Hackney, a very deep well had been sunk many years ago, and covered over with wood, which had become so rotten that the whole surface of the ground gave way, at least 18 feet in circumference; and fell into the well, which was at the smallest computation 40 feet deep. The Commissioners of Sewers of the Metropolitan Trust, have been made acquainted with all the facts and urgently requested to have the well covered with brick and stone, so as to prevent a recurrence of such a frightful accident for the future.; but I regret to say they have totally disregarded the application, and again, in the midst of a thoroughfare often crowded, merely placed on top of this frightful well a few boards covered with gravel. Perhaps, Sir, you may think the narrative of sufficient importance to call forth your able assistance in the cause of the public, by telling the commissioners to do their duty; or by the neglect of it, the next sinking in of one of their wells may be attended with consequences of a more dreadful nature. I beg to add, there are six or seven wells in the same street and should any of them be in the same rotten state, the lives of the passengers are in great jeopardy.

I am Sir, your respectively,
W. Grant   London-field, Hackney.

Mare Street looking north towards the old church, from near the future junction with Graham Road, *c.* 1840.

Births, Marriages and Deaths

26 October 1742

Wednesday Mr Pratt, an eminent Merchant of this City, was married at Hackney to Miss Glanville of Mark-lane, a young Lady of great Merit, with a Fortune of £10,000.

7 January 1744

. . . The same Day was married at Hackney, Mr Clever, an eminent and wealthy Distiller at Mile End, to Miss Sally Robinson of Hackney; a young Lady of excellent Accomplishments, with a Fortune of £7000.

October 1751

Last Tuesday Night died at his House at Hackney, Jacob Mendez de Costa, sen. Formerly an eminent Merchant, reputed to be worth £70000, acquired with the fairest of Characters, as is evident by his extensive Charity, a Virtue which is not to be found in the griping Usurer, the Modern Trickster, nor the extravagant Scraper, in whom the Extremes of Prodigality and Avarice centre: His Benevolence was felt by all necessitous Objects, Christians as well as Jews; it being his Maxim, that all the Seed of Adam were Brothers, and entitled to each others good Offices, how much soever they may differ in religious Principles.

1775

A whimsical Lady at Hackney, who some years ago had her coffin made under the persuasion that she should not live long, and had it placed in her living room, was yesterday married to a young fellow, and coffin sent back to the undertaker.

5 January 1792

On Sunday, an Elopement took place from a Boarding School at Hackney. – The parties were a young lady of seventeen, who, on coming of age, will be entitled to a considerable fortune, and a Naval Officer of Subaltern Rank. They are supposed to have directed their course to Scotland – but before notice could be given to the friends of the young Lady, were probably beyond the reach of pursuit.

21 September 1821, Sudden Death

A female, aged upwards of 70 years, has resided for a considerable time in a small house at Cambridge-heath, Hackney-road. She kept no servant, associated with none of her neighbours and the only inmate was a favourite cat. Her doors and windows were constantly kept secured, and the signal of the milk-man, or anyone applying for admission, was throwing a stone against the door or window. A neighbour's daughter was in the habit of going every morning to procure her water, but on Monday, after repeated signals, she could get no entrance. The girl went for her mother, and with a diamond ring they cut a pane of glass, got admission, and proceeded upstairs. There they found the old lady, by the side of her bed, with her clothes on, and a small piece of cat's meat in her hand. They soon discovered she was dead. It is supposed she died of apoplexy, as no marks of violence appeared, nor was any of the property disturbed. From the abstemious manner of her living it was supposed that her circumstances were very limited, but on examining her drawers, Stock Receipts and Government Securities were found to the amount of near One Hundred Thousand Pounds! She always declared she would make no will, for 'the King' should have all her money. Every search has been made, but no will found. Her sister died a few years ago and left her £7000, which, it now seems, she at first declined, saying she was not in want of money. No relative has yet appeared. She was a maiden lady, and her name Sarah Bond.

It was later reported that Sarah Bond had a strong dislike of men and women. She was one of the four daughters of a jeweller who had lived in an alley leading from Wellclose Square to the Ratcliffe highway, who died in about 1770, dividing his property between Sarah and her surviving sister. The sister died in about 1800 and left £600 to Sarah, who bought an annuity of £750 p.a. and then invested further savings in £13,000 of 3 per cents, £1,000 in four per cents and £150 p.a. in long annuities. It was thought that the likely recipient would be a Mr Bond, a butcher in Shoreditch, who claimed to be her second cousin, but he failed to find the church where her mother and father were married. One Theophilus Bond also attempted to make a claim, but without success. She still remained unburied at the end of October, as the Lord Chancellor's approval had not been forthcoming.

EDUCATION

1791

At Mrs Larkham's School at Dalston (a pleasant and healthful Village between Kingsland and Hackney), young Ladies are genteelly and well boarded, and taught all Kinds of useful and fashionable Needlework, the English and French Languages

The Infant Orphan Asylum, Dalston Lane (on the site of the north entrance to the German Hospital). From a watercolour by George Hawkins, 1836.

grammatically, Geography, the use of the Globes, History, and several other Branches of necessary and polite Learning, at 18 guineas a Year. No Entrance. Writing, Dancing, Musick and Drawing, by able Masters. Lest any Prejudice should attend the School, in Consequence of the Lowness of the Price, or this Mode of making it known, Mrs Larkham thinks it may not be improper to observe, that, in order to give her Scholars every advantage, with Respect to Accommodation as well as Improvement, the Number is limited to 20. Viands of the best Kinds are provided in great Plenty. In addition to her own stated Attendance in the School, she has the Assistance of a Teacher of distinguished Abilities. Writing, Arithmetic, English Grammar, Geography, Use of Globes, History etc are taught by Mr Larkham. Dancing, Drawing, and Musick are taught by Masters of Eminence in their several Professions. In few Words, Mrs Larkham hopes she may venture to say, without being deemed guilty of Ostentation, that as great Care will be taken of the young Ladies in Point of Board, Education, Health and orals, as at any School in the Kingdom. Cards of Reference may be had to Families of the highest Respectability, who have Daughters at the School. The School will be opened on Monday the 16th January.

WAR AND POLITICS

1773

Monday a duel was fought in a field near Hoxton. Occasioned by a political dispute, between a Clerk belonging to a public-office and a Liveryman who had polled for

Mr Wilkes, wherein the former was run through the body, and now lies at the point of death.

August 1793

A few days ago Mr Breillat, Pump-maker, in Hackney road, was committed to Newgate, for having made use of seditious and inflammatory language; 'that he wishes the French would land 100,000 in England to fight against the Government party.' Other expressions of the like tendency were fully proved to have been uttered by him, prior to his merited commitment to durance vile. Notice was given by Mr White, solicitor for the Crown, that 24 hour notice of bail should be given to him before it would be accepted.

Breillat was bailed for the sum of £200 to appear at the next quarter sessions.

15 February 1797

In the Napoleonic Wars local militia soon gained a reputation for bumbling incompetence. This case came before the Clerkenwell magistrates:

Mr Sylvester [prosecuting] stated That the Defendant, Thomas, together with five others of the names of Dore, Barratt, Downing, Ward and Windsor, were Members of an Associated Body in the vicinity of Hackney in the County of Middlesex; and who have embodied themselves for the immediate purpose of preserving the peace of the Country from the invasion of its enemies, foreign or domestic; they had denominated

The Lamb and Flag public house, December 1946.

themselves 'The Hackney Association Volunteers' and being resolutely determined to mark their characters for some great feat of bravery, unluckily fell into the desperate battle he was about to describe, and which, he lamented, could not be determined on the field of combat, and therefore had become the province of a Jury to decide.

It appeared that on the 25th day of October last, these renowned Veterans had a grand field-day and after being reviewed by their Captain, they were dismissed and a great number of them adjourned to a dinner provided on the occasion at the house of one John Gattenby, the sign of the Lamb, at Homerton. In the afternoon, the Prosecutor, Simon (a native of Jersey), came into the house, accompanied by his Nephew, who called for a tankard of porter, and during the conversation which took place they were joined by Thomas and Dore, two of the above Defendants, who were equipped in all the gay pomp of their uniform; in this conversation, it was that these soldiers discovered, from Simon's dialect, that he could not be an Englishman, and therefore concluded that he must be a Frenchman. It was on this account the quarrel began. They considered it to be their duty to guard against the common enemy. Simon denied being a Frenchman, but all would not do; a violent scuffle ensued, and violent blows were dealt on both sides. Thomas and Dore were joined by the other Defendants and several other persons who were at the dinner, and belonged to the Association. It appeared however, that Simon had, in the course of the affray, picked up a stick, with which he so belaboured the soldiers, that the Court considered that he ought, on that account to be satisfied and recommended that the matter go no further.

CHAPTER THREE

EVENTS AND THE LOCAL SCENE

Local papers have always carried historical pieces, both on contemporary archaeological finds and reflections on aspects of Hackney's past.

A find was reported in the local press on 22 September 1933 as a result of the construction of the first Powell House estate.

RELICS UNEARTHED AT CLAPTON

Persons of an antiquarian turn of mind have been wondering whether the excavations carried out on the site of the proposed municipal tenements in Lower Clapton-road would bring to light anything of interest. They have not been disappointed, though the use of modern appliances is not so favourable to such discoveries as the old method of digging and delving. Beneath the foundations of Byland House (the home of the Powells – a branch of the Baden-Powell family) has been unearthed an old brickwork chamber containing a large quantity of damaged glass and bottles. Two perfect specimens of wine bottles, about eight inches high have been rescued and the British Museum authorities have fixed the date of these as being about 1680. Possibly therefore, the old under-

Byland House, Lower Clapton Road, *c.* 1930.

ground chamber was the wine cellar of an older mansion, demolished to make way for Byland House, built about the year 1700. . . . The probability is that the relics will find a home in the Hackney Central Library with other local souvenirs of the past.

Byland House may have been substantially rebuilt by James Powell in the late eighteenth century and it is conceivable that the house could have been constructed in the late seventeenth century.

Substantial changes were being made in the area during November 1902, though not for the better according to one local reporter:

The neighbourhood of Dalston has undergone many changes in recent years. Slowly but surely its rural aspect is disappearing under the ruthless hand of the modern builder, and older residents will recall with regret the once pleasant gardens and nursery grounds which here abounded. All but one, if I remember rightly, these latter have been swept away. The gardens too, are vanishing, one by one. Several of them have been covered by villa residences and these, in turn have had to make way for huge blocks of flats. More of these unsightly buildings, I hear, are about to be erected opposite Wayland-avenue in Dalston-lane, by the Guiness Trust. . . .

In Lower Clapton-road, too, changes are in progress which will materially alter the aspect of the locality. The two large houses occupied for so many years by the Young Women's Christian Association have been razed to the ground and in their place will be erected a new police station as headquarters of the 'J' division. The old station in Mare Street will disappear . . . the Y.W.C.A has migrated to Kenninghall-road where commodious premises have been secured. . . .

The housebreakers have also been busy in yet another part of our district and their operations here can scarcely be regarded with disfavour. At Shoreditch the old almshouses facing the Town Hall have disappeared . . . to make room for a new police station and a new police court. The station will replace the Hoxton police station in the Kingsland-road, which has long been found inadequate. . . . The police court will relieve the pressure on the North London and Worship-street courts. . . . [I]n the view of the occasionally explosive nature of proceedings at the Town Hall, there is something grimly appropriate in the fact that a police-station, court and cells are to be planted in such close proximity.

A small part of lost Homerton was remembered by H. Burdon, recalling the early 1880s in a local paper on 17 April 1935.

Healthy Terrace was a spot adjacent to the 'Adam and Eve' public house, opposite the Hackney Infirmary. It possessed an ideal tea garden, for one could gaze across acres of farmland. A short footpath by the side of an ancient red-brick wall covered with rank ivy led you to a sign with the words 'Teas provided' and a small tea garden of the country type, enclosed with bushes and laurels, in which were arranged a number of forms painted green and one or two rustic tables. There were many flowers growing among intersected paths and here people might take tea and look in the direction of the winding Lea beyond, with a fair view of the Sewardstone Hills in the distance.

High-street [Homerton] at this time still retained some of its early Georgian characteristics, and the old-world aspect is still pictured in my memory. The path led past the tea garden and fizzled out in a meadow beyond. Old country carts laden with farm produce from Low Leyton, and heaped high at times with hay and straw, rumbled up Marsh-hill into Hummerton – for such was the early 18th century name of this place – a fact confirmed by the finding of an old earthenware beer mug, dug up during the demolition of a hedgerow on the hillside immediately beyond 'Turpin's House'. The inscription on this utensil was 'Ye Grayhounde, Hummerton, 1750'.

Healthy Terrace (the ends of these cottages are visible on the left) and the southern part of Pratt's Lane, Homerton, *c.* 1870. Oil painting by Walter Burnett, 1912.

Looking from Healthy-terrace in the direction of what is now Chatsworth-road was a footpath leading from Brooksby's-walk down to Pond-lane. This path divided farm produce lands, and I recall seeing cartloads of rhubarb one Spring morning being carted away for market. During the summer dwarf runner beans were cultivated in profusion and attracted myriads of bees, while the bloom was about them. Then one day came the spoiler with pick and shovel and 'Sleepy Hollow' was no more.

In the Hackney Mercury *of 4 July 1885, the starting point for a piece by 'H.C.' was an engraving of Hackney in 1840, which was for sale in the window of a photographer's shop near Clapton Square. This included the King's Head, then recently demolished. The author describes the Mare Street of his day on a Saturday night when the street market was at its height, beginning with the right-hand side of the road, where:*

One or two of the drapers adopt early closing and in front of their shops are generally to be seen women and girls selling flowers; the gay products of the gardens and fields presenting a very different appearance to the dresses of the vendors. . . . Two or three of the flower dealers apparently belong to a family or group, for while one is offering a 'tempting handful' or a 'button-hole' to customers, another is in a corner or lay-by, with the stock basket, arranging other posies. . . . The shops on this side of the way appear to do a fair amount of business on Saturday night; but as most of them are of a 'select' character, their principal trade has probably been done earlier in the day, when careful housewives who do not have to wait until the afternoon or evening for their week's money, have done their shopping and . . . have gone out for an airing to some place of amusement. A very considerable number of the housewives of the future however, and their admirers, make Mare-street their promenade on Saturday, as on other evenings, especially Sunday.

Mare Street from the junction with Graham Road, 1887. Photograph by Alfred Braddock.

Crossing over by Morning-lane for the purpose of returning stationwards, it may be seen that it is here that the real business of Saturday night marketing begins. At the corner of the lane there is much brightness shed around by the china shop, which not very high, is lit from top to bottom. . . . Among the 'gutter merchants' stationed here is almost inevitably to be found one with a pile of watercresses, . . . which calls up a recollection of . . . when there were flourishing beds of the wholesome plant few yards off, but where now there is quite a colony of houses and not a trace of garden save in front of some quaint little habitations, the occupants of which take a delight in attending to their strips of ground. . . . Passing on one cannot fail to notice the number of flowers stalls. . . . Articles of a more material nature however are in smart requisition and the cry of 'All that lot of pinks for a penny – a market bunch' . . . Is mingled with 'Fine berries, tuppence a full quart'. . . . A step or two further on there is a stall heaped with lettuce and cucumbers, the former being cut open to show the solid white heart; and nearby is another stall whose speciality is rhubarb, in huge bundles, the owner of which recommends it as he thrusts a heap before a customer 'there, that will break your wrist'. . . . At a little distance a girl is selling bunches of mint (at a halfpenny each) fit to go with green peas on a stall hard by, with the joint of lamb that is being bargained for at a butcher's close by one's elbow, or to be dried for winter use in pea soup – 'always handy' as the girl says herself. Then there are stalls for the sale of fish, wet and dry, the latter being represented by bloaters, spitted on long rods, something like you see in curing-houses at Yarmouth; and great haddocks, hung up so as to be shown to best advantage, the stalls having coverings. The 'fish interest' is represented by a stand on which there are little saucers of whelks . . . but . . . in Hackney the dealers in these molluscs do not set them out in tempting array as they do in Shoreditch, where

24

fantastic shapes are formed with the shells, while the contents are garnished with parsley etc.

Utility is the main characteristic of the Mare-street market, but the fanciful is not quite neglected . . . by means of a board or two devoted to children, toys and cheap nick-nacks being here obtainable, but a thoroughly business-like air hangs over all and humour is conspicuous by its absence. . . .

At present however the place is rather inconvenient and even dangerously crowded for this is one of the most awkward . . . parts of Mare-street, there being scarcely room for a person to pass between the stalls and the tramway cars.

Street-widening would have helped, though perhaps not if it displaced the stall-holders, who might, as in Chatsworth Road, have assisted the trade of the shop-keepers. But 'H.C.' was relieved to get away from the crowds on Mare Street and into the tree-lined churchyard.

Another journalist, George R. Sims, concentrated on the evening parades, which just before the composition of his piece for the Strand Magazine *in 1904 had been the focus of some trouble. This is an edited version from the original text:*

Mare street is famous for its Monkey Parades. On Sunday evenings it is packed from end to end with promenaders. It is the predominance of the boy and girl element that has given it a reputation for monkey business.

There are plenty of people on the pavement and in the roadway. Here and there are groups of typical London lads, cane, cap and cigarette. Whatever they have been in the past, they have no apish tricks now. Of tumult and disorder, even at the hour when the crowd was greatest, there was no sign. I expected scratchbacks and playful punchings and an exchange of sallies between the sexes. There was nothing of the sort.

And yet the scene was remarkable, for there was considerably more young women than men, and the majority of the young women promenaded in twos, occasionally in threes. Their costumes were gay and gorgeous as the costumes that grace the Hampstead Heath on a Whit Monday. The favourite colours were petunia, violet, green and sky-blue. Two young ladies, one dark and one fair, had adorned them-selves in light green blouses, red hats and blue skirts and waistbands of bright yellow. Another pair were in costumes of aggressively bright blue and wore with them heliotrope hats. When the scene was at its busiest, Mare Street was absolutely prismatic. But the blues and greens, violets and yellows were not in merging lines; they broke up and intermixed in a kaleidoscope of coloured bits that was at times

The 'Monkey Parade' along Mare Street.

absolutely dazzling. Occasionally a weird effect was added to the daring schemes of colour by looping the skirt with an old fashioned dress suspender, which fastens round the waist and catches up the dress in bunches by means of a clasp.

This is all in contrast with Hackney Downs, which Sims found respectable and subdued with the middle-aged and the newly married strolling side by side; in the latter case with the husband wheeling the pram. This was in contrast to the experience of a local Presbyterian minister, whose account is in Chapter Six.

The Boer War saw an outburst of patriotism, which was also drawn on to raise funds and have a good time in a charitable cause. This is an edited report from the Hackney Gazette *for 22 June 1900:*

HACKNEY CARNIVAL PROCESSION – AN IMPOSING PAGEANT

Hackney has made its great effort on behalf of the widows and orphans of those who have fallen in South Africa. Never before has Hackney risen to the occasion so splendidly. Politics are forgotten and members of both parties worked energetically together to assist the grand cause.

All along the various lines of the route the scene was an animated and a gay one. The Town Hall reflected much credit upon S.J. Rose, the Engineer at the baths. Centre piece was the Queen's Head, illuminated with eighty electric lights; around her Majesty were arranged the leading generals now serving at the front, while all along the front of the building were electric and coloured balloons – red, white and blue – and under the porch was a basket of pretty electric flowers.

Even in the poorest neighbourhood, and even in the poorest house in it, some sort of display of flags, draperies or lanterns has been made.

A sketch from the programme of the 1900 Hackney Carnival. The artist has chosen to show the reverse side of the banner.

The Hackney Board of Guardians at the ceremony to lay the foundation of the workhouse extension, 1889. The degree of good cheer at Christmas depended on these men.

Amongst the most striking of the procession of ornamental cars was the beautiful car, 'our Empire' by Messrs Matthew Rose and Son, in which the United Kingdom (represented by ladies) was defended by both arms of the service; the Time of Peace Coach representing a typical English cottage and garden with the old man and his wife and baby very comfortable and contented – an embattled corner of Mafeking, by the Reform Club; the Belles of Hackney, by Mr Capon; a hunting car, with hounds; the fiery eyed pig in Mr Harris' 'sausage' kingly chariot; the Druids with sickle and mistletoe; and a charming Sylvan realisation of a gipsy encampment with fire alight and pot astew.

The crowd were most well behaved too; we shouted at every opportunity our determination never to submit to the yoke. We blessed our Queen and cheered our heroes till we could cheer no more. And be it said that we gave our pennies freely.

Victorian workhouses were intended to deter the poor and left an indelible mark of fear on a generation of working-class people of ending their days in one. The grimmer side of workhouse life is touched upon in Chapter Four, but workhouses also featured in sentimental seasonal pieces. This edited extract from a local paper of 27 December 1901, describes an early Edwardian workhouse. After detailing the preparation of virtually 2 tons of Christmas pudding and noting that while there would be no beers for the inhabitants, there would be plentiful supplies of coffee, mineral waters, fruit, sweets, nuts, tobacco and snuff and extra tea and sugar, the reporter described the dining room:

A JOLLY CHRISTMAS. TONS OF ROAST BEEF AND PLUM PUDDING AT HACKNEY

Several of the male inhabitants took great pains in wreathing evergreens tastefully about the columns and windows, while Miss Spratley, the labour mistress . . . arranged no end of pretty flowers. . . . Several large mottoes expressed the good feeling of the season. . . . At the entrance hangs an old trophy, a plum pudding in picture, done by a former inmate.

Every ward was decorated on a similar scale. A peep into one of the men's day rooms revealed some remarkably clever and patriotic colours that would be an ornament to any drawing room. The designer in chief was a plasterer, a comparatively young man with one leg disabled, who relieves the tedium of the daily round with carving. . . .

Inmates also received gifts of toys and sweets, tobacco and cigars, a musical box for the old people's ward and, from the wife of a Guardian, 53 pairs of woollen cuffs.

The death of Queen Victoria on 22 January 1901 marked the end of the century and of an era. This report comes from the Hackney Standard *of 25 January 1901:*

The sad news reached Hackney about seven o-clock; soon the bells of various churches tolled; and everyone became acquainted with the fact that the Queen was no more. The town's meeting adjourned directly a vote of condolence had been carried in solemn silence; a concert in the manor Theatre was adjourned, the Dalston and Alexandra Theatre were closed by order of the Lord Chamberlain; a first rate entertainment in All Saints hall arranged by Mr George Hogsflesh, was abandoned directly the news was reached. . . .

On Wednesday morning national mourning was to be seen on every side. Tradesmen either lowered their blinds and put up familiar black board; many private houses had their blinds drawn; at the Town Hall the flag was lowered at the various clubs. . . . The various drapery and hosiery establishments immediately dressed their windows in black and must have done a great trade. Nearly everyone is wearing black or dark clothes – for it is indeed a case of National mourning for one who had endeared herself to all. . . .

In advance of the coronation of Edward VII national King's Dinners for the Poor were organized and funded by local efforts in July 1902. Hackney's Mayor for the year, Walter Johnson, claimed to have visited 15,000 guests at events spread across all the local wards. Events at St Luke's Church, Sidney Road Board School, Morley Hall, the Eton Mission, Hackney Wick, Matthias Road Board Schools and the Mildmay Radical Club were all accompanied by entertainment – 500 guests at the Matthias Road schools each received a coronation mug, while over 400 at the Mildmay Club were treated to trapeze artists, a mimic and a comedian. The coronation itself took place in August 1902. This report covers one local street party:

BECK ROAD, HACKNEY, ON CORONATION NIGHT

Beck Road is one of the quiet respectable well-to-do side streets running into Mare street, Hackney. All the houses could be let ten times over and people who want to take one have to wait months before a chance occurs to enter upon occupation. The appearance of a notice 'House to Let', would bring a crowd of neighbours out as quickly as a house on fire.

The occupiers are anxious that their relatives should come and live near them. . . . This has introduced a kind of clannishness . . . To which we may add loyalty, which on Coronation night was very marked. Houses were decorated with flags . . . and fairy lamps which was only the prelude to the evening of entertainment which . . . lasted til the first hour of Sunday. . . .

At one house on the south side of the street near the railway arch, a happy party had assembled. The heads of several families, their wives, grandfathers and grandmothers and blooming young ladies and their probable life partners were all present. . . .

One young man fingered the keys of the piano as if his digits had electric current in them. The effect was electrical upon the young ladies also, They danced and danced without exhaustion, and then went at it again. . . . Neighbours, when some stentorian voice rolled out the words of a well-known and popular song, came to the doors to listen and enjoy themselves. And this is how the residents of one of the many little respectable streets of the ancient Borough of Hackney kept Coronation night.

Clarnico, the confectionery manufacturers of Hackney Wick, had their own fire brigade, ambulance service and brass band and held an open day to publicize their achievements. This report of an inspection by the brigade superintendent of St John's Ambulance comes from a local paper of July 1901:

. . . There was a large attendance of members of the firm, workpeople and the general public. The large buildings were gaily decorated with flags and streamers . . . whilst the comfort of all present was studied by the handing round of suitable refreshments. . . .

The Clarnico fire engine, 1904.

After a selection of music played by the excellent band, the display commenced. . . . A shrill sound from the commander's whistle brought smartly attired firemen from all parts of the works to attack a supposed outbreak in the Caramel Building. Hose and fire truck were soon got into operation, while the firm's ambulance men were on the spot to succour those who had fallen in the execution of duty. Down the long flight of steps came the injured. . . . Stretchers were in readiness and bandages applied here to a head and there to an arm, whilst broken legs were promptly 'splintered'.

After the 'victims' were taken away to hospital there was a march past of the various sections, a tug of war between all three sections – which the bandsmen won and another fire on the far side of the Regent's Canal.

At the end of the same month the brigade may have been among those called to an incident on their own doorstep. On Saturday 27 July 1901 there was a very heavy rainstorm in north-east London. The water caused the naphtha tanks of Capel Carless and Leonard, petrol and spirit refiners, to overflow. The naphtha ran under the gates of the yard and down White Post Lane, where it settled on top of flood water standing on the street.

The inmates of the tenements all unmindful of the proximity of a great peril, were sheltering from the storm when, at a quarter past six o-clock, there was a very loud report, a tremendous crash of shattered glass, and a great burst of fierce flame all down White Post-lane. By some extraordinary means, which has not up to the present been ascertained, the naphtha had been ignited and exploded. The immediate effects . . . were to wreck the fronts of eleven houses in White Post-lane and the fire that followed ignited the buildings.

The terrified occupants of the houses, several of whom had sustained serious injuries by the explosion . . . rushed out of the burning houses and into the flooded street to find that they were surrounded by fire and were breathing in an atmosphere which was noxious with the fumes of the naphtha.

Extraordinarily only one family were seriously hurt, as their house, No. 76, was totally wrecked, and one of them died. But the article added that twelve of the seventeen families affected were uninsured, and though they were only renting the property, they would lose all their possessions. The firm's liability was clearly regarded by the reporter as limited or non-existent.

Local action to help the unemployed during the depression of the 1930s also made the local press. On 30 May 1932, the Hackney Gazette *and* North London Advertiser *ran an editorial on the work of Shoreditch's Juvenile Advisory Committee, which was working with the employment exchange and had helped place 3,580 boys and girls in jobs. On 11 January 1933 it carried this report on another local initiative:*

THE UNEMPLOYMENT PROBLEM
Centre opened at Hoxton
Hoxton's first bid to tackle the local employment problem on the lines of mutual service advocated by the Prince of Wales was made yesterday when the new S.O.S (Scheme of Service) centre at 3 Hemsworth-street was officially opened by Mr W. Arnot Morton, the chairman of the committee responsible for the project.

The Hoxton workshop for the unemployed, 1933.

Five rooms were available for the unemployed for occupational work, but two rooms could also be used for recreation. From about three dozen, the membership had grown to fifty men and they themselves had undertaken the conversion work, making new staircases, fireplaces, ceilings, floors and cupboards.

Provision is being made for unemployed carpenters, tailors, bootmakers and others, who will be supplied with materials to satisfy the various needs of their colleagues. They will not receive any payment – the essence of the scheme being voluntary service – and goods will not be sold on the open market.

As a contemporary report in a national paper made plain, if one member came in with a pair of his child's shoes to mend, then the S.O.S would supply the materials, and the shoe-mender member the labour. Simple food and drink was also provided at cost price. Labour could be exchanged for other labour so that carpenters making up sheds for allotment holders would be 'paid' in vegetables.

Among those involved in organizing the scheme were Dr Donald Soper, then minister of Islington Central Hall, the matron of the nearby Sun Babies Nursery and Mr Bellamy of Hoxton Hall. It was intended that the men should take on the running of the centre themselves and eventually make it self supporting.

A similar initiative was launched in Hackney in the same month, intending to use an empty factory in Silesia Buildings, off Mare Street, supported by donations from local people and businesses.

Between 13 and 25 May 1957 traders in Ridley Road market celebrated thirty years as a licensed market. It originated in Kingsland High Street and was flourishing in August 1870, when the Hackney Gazette *reported on the sale of a great quantity of haddock that were not fit for human consumption. In 1901 Hackney Council determined to use the*

Gandhi visited the East End during his trip to England in 1931 to discuss home rule for India at the Round Table conference. His visit included an engagement at Kingsley Hall, Bow, where he received a present of oranges from one of the children of Hoxton's Pearly King, 16 September 1931.

repaving of the High Street with wooden blocks to clear it of stall-holders and move the costers to a side street. Prosecutions ensued in March and April 1901, though it was not until February 1902 that over seventy costers lost a case at the North London police court and the Council succeeded. The traders moved to Ridley Road on an informal basis prior to the grant of a licence. This is an edited account of a piece that appeared in the Hackney Gazette *on 10 May 1957:*

'The market has been in existence for more like 50 years,' said Mr G.W. Webster, organiser of the Ridley-road Traders Association. . . . 'There used to be stalls at the top of the road at Kingsland High-street'. But listen to John 'Buster' Cain, who together with his 67-year-old mother, runs a salad and vegetable stall in the centre of the market. 'My father was one of the first traders here', he told the Gazette, 'He used to tell how years before it became a licensed market, all the traders stood at one end of the road with their goods under their arms waiting for a policeman to blow his whistle. At that signal they used to race into Ridley-road and stake their pitch.'

Cain won the George Medal for rescuing 137 people from a shelter at a Dalston paint factory in 1940. Running a stall involved being up all night in advance

A.E. Craft by his stall in Ridley Road market, in the 1930s.

of big events, like Christmas. Another stall-holder, Charlie Morris, started thirty-four years before and:

. . . had to pawn property to raise the money to start a stall. . . . Now he has worked up to three confectionery shops employing seven people. 'I used to auction chocolates near here when Ridley-road was all houses with no shops'. . . . All his stories stress the earnest desire of the traders to earn a living by giving customers a fair deal: 'Things that cost 9½d lb in my shop, for instance, cost 8d per quarter in shops outside the market', he declared. . . .

A number of famous people have worked in the market. It has often been the setting for many films and documentaries. Among the celebrities was Jack Solomons, top boxing promoter, who used to go to work at a fishmonger's. His brother, Max, who now runs the business, said 'Jack still retains an interest. He phones every day for news of the market. He likes the place and the people.' . . .

The celebrations included a number of promotional events, including prizes of a large-screen television set and a weekend for two in Paris.

Something out of this world made news for the Hackney Gazette *on 24 November 1970:*

FLYING SAUCER OVER HACKNEY?
Ministry investigates
Yesterday the Ministry of Defence was investigating a reported sighting of an unidentified flying object over Hackney. Mr Douglas Lockhart, a 32-year-old freelance journalist of 97 Downs Park-road told the Gazette. 'It was seen by myself and two others at 11.35, Saturday night . . . it glided across an almost clear sky at a height of not more than three thousand feet'.

He claimed that the object – 'clearly visible and seemingly large' – had a yellow-orange nucleus, a black oval outline, was surrounded by a corona of red light which looked like a flame and was totally silent.

The other people who saw it, he said, were Maureen Boyle, a secretary and Brian Haddon, who live at the same address. 'Maureen saw it out of the window and told me. I did not think it was a normal aircraft and we went out into the street,' he said 'When our strange visitor stopped, changed direction and headed back towards us, Maureen ran back into the house for another witness. When Mr Haddon, who lives upstairs, arrived, the glowing visitor, now only an orange ball of light slowly zig-zagged its way off . . . and finally disappeared.'

Lockhart had seen three orange triangles over Coatbridge in Scotland ten years earlier. Hackney police were suitably tight lipped: said a spokesman at Hackney police station, 'Nobody reported a UFO to us'. According to the Gazette, *Mr Lockhart later appeared on ITV's* Today *programme and was interviewed again outside his flat.*

National stories also impinged on the locality. In June 1975 one Paul Daniels, described by the Hackney Gazette *as Hackney's 'Corporal Blimp' and founder of a 2,000-strong army, was asked to recruit for the Rhodesian army. Stoke Newington had more than its share of excitement in December 1975 when police raided an IRA bomb factory. This report came from the* Hackney Gazette *of 19 December 1975:*

CROSSED LINE PINPOINTED IRA BOMB FACTORY

A frightened mother exclusively told the 'Gazette' this week how IRA terrorists in Stoke Newington threatened to kill her teenage son after he heard them discussing bombing plans.

The boy was ringing from his home to his mother's work place when he got a crossed line. He listened . . . and heard two Irishmen talking about a bombing attack. He was threatened 'We'll get you.'

Scotland Yard moved in and tapped the family's phone. They continually rang the number in a bid to get another crossed line. It was this incredible stroke of luck which pinned down the location of the bomb factory to Stoke Newington.

A crowd outside the Milton Road house used by the IRA as a bomb factory, 1975.

After a tip off from another local person, police swooped on the top floor four room flat at 99 Milton Grove – an early Victorian house. The bathroom was booby-trapped with a bomb when the police entered.

They found 'a significant quantity' of timing devices and detonators hidden under a bath and stacked in a kitchen cupboard. Scotland Yard warned there could be other terrorists' hide-aways in the Stoke Newington area and everyone should be on the lookout. The landlord of the house . . . has gone into hiding, fearing for his life.

Abney Park Cemetery was founded in 1838, but the sale of plots in perpetuity contributed to a steady decline in income, which by 1975 had become terminal. This report is from the Hackney Gazette *for 25 April 1975.*

JUNGLE WARNING AS CEMETERY OWNERS GO BANKRUPT

The seriously neglected Abney Park Cemetery in Stoke Newington will soon become a 'graveyard jungle' warned local playwright Nemone Lethbridge this week. She added, 'This cemetery is already extremely overgrown and during the summer it'll be like an equatorial forest'.

But Mrs Lethbridge, who has been leading a 'clean-up-the-cemetery'' campaign for several months, believes that the park is in no worse a state now than it was last year, even though the leaseholders, Chingford Mount Cemetery Company have gone bankrupt. The company went bust on January 20 and since then the cemetery has not been maintained. The owners, Bank and Commercial Holdings, are not obligated by law to clean up the cemetery and neither are the Department of the Environment.

Abney Park
Cemetery, 1975.

Distressed relatives complained of graves left open after funerals, but the official receiver's spokesman claimed that nothing could be done until an official liquidator was appointed.

Mrs Lethbridge called on Hackney Council to accept responsibility for maintaining the cemetery. 'This is a golden opportunity for them to show some public spirit', she said 'Nothing has been done to the cemetery for the past three years and when it becomes warmer, it'll be graveyard jungle.' And Mrs Lethbridge said that graves were not being filled in even when the leaseholders were a viable company.

A town hall spokesman said 'The council have no authority at this stage to maintain the cemetery.'

However, Hackney Council did step in and acquired the cemetery for £1 in 1978. It is now managed by the Abney Park Cemetery Trust, a descendant of the campaigning group in which Nemone Lethbridge was active.

CHAPTER FOUR

HOUSING, HEALTH AND WELFARE

HOUSING

Until the 1960s the bulk of the housing in what is now the London Borough of Hackney was rented and in turn tenants with leases often let out rooms. The following cautionary tale appeared in the Hackney Gazette *on 2 October 1869:*

ANOTHER CAUTION TO LETTERS OF LODGINGS

Sir – There is a class of Jeremy Diddlers of whom it behoves the above to beware. They dress trim and neat and try to ape the manners of gentlemen without possessing the means; they will wait on you with a polite bow, and perhaps hand you a neat card engraved 'Fortescue Fitzfungus,' Esq. Or some other snobbish cogonomen. But don't be humbugged. 'Fair spoken phrases, graced with a courtier's bow are very pleasant things, but rarely hold much more of grateful truths than the bright shine that cunning reptiles spread to catch their prey.' There is a little knot of these worthies in Dalston, who assist each other in fleecing their landladies by impressing them with an idea of their important connexions [*sic*]. They are very chary of giving you their place of business in the 'City', because, when they get as deep in your debt as your good nature allows, it enables them to double and throw you off the scent, when it is time to apply for the assistance of the county court.

My advice is, in all cases insist upon having proper and bone fide references from parties in search of lodgings, be satisfied that they are correct, and above all know their position in life and their place of business. By observing these rules we shall, in great measure, spoil the little game of these pests of society, who live by their cunning and fatten on the good nature and credulity of their dupes.

Yours etc, Outpost.

The first municipal housing schemes in Hackney were drawn up in the last years of the nineteenth century by the London County Council. The newly created Hackney Borough Council planned a project of its own in Lee Place, just south of Clapton station. Mr J. Godfrey, presumably a Clapton resident, wrote to a local paper outlining his objections in March 1901. After outlining the proposed scheme to put up working-class dwellings at a cost of £84,000, he described the site:

The greater part of the frontage is now occupied by three large houses, built 55 years ago. On the opposite frontage there are four large detached villas, built 38 years ago. These four houses are at the present time as valuable and as good residential property as any in the parish.

. . . on the north side [of the three houses] there is a private lane leading down to what has been a brickfield for 35 years, out of which the brick earth has been dug to an average depth of about 20 feet and filled with all kinds of rubbish carted from the City and elsewhere. Although it is now filled up, the board at the entrance to the lane still remains up, inviting carmen to come and shoot their rubbish there.

Godfrey then goes on to claim that the site is not worth the price asked of contractors and that there is very little slum property in Hackney. What there is is situated in Homerton, Hackney Wick and parts of South Hackney, and the 4,000 overcrowded persons living there do not pay rents that would meet the real costs of the proposed housing, quoting the deputy Mayor who had said 'There is little hope of artisan dwellings paying'.

Then again, should they carry out their Clapton scheme and bring the people from Homerton, Hackney Wick and South Hackney, do they propose to buy property and pull it down and carry out another scheme, or are they going to allow the people from the real slum property in the East-end of London to come and take the places of these persons they have provided new tenements for at Clapton?

The expense, Godfrey feels, is not justified and any municipal housing schemes should be left to the London County Council.

But in the event both the LCC and the boroughs established successful programmes to build housing, although it was not until well after the First World War that they were able to provide it at a cost the poorest could afford. Much of the nineteenth-century housing stock in some areas, notably Shoreditch, was in poor condition by the late 1930s, when the Shoreditch Housing Association published 'Growing up in Shoreditch'. This is how it was reviewed in August 1938:

Growing up in Shoreditch is a grim business for the average child according to the Shoreditch Housing Association Ltd. The detailed results of an investigation into the lives of 400 of the children selected at random, as revealed in a pamphlet just issued

Councillor J.S. Baker, Mayor of Shoreditch, waiting his turn at the Hoxton Sun Babies Nursery, which served one of the poorer areas of the borough, October 1934.

Postwar life – the backs of houses in Shaftesbury Street, Shoreditch, with the bomb-damaged ruins of a factory in the foreground, 1946.

by the association, show what still remains to be done in 1938, despite desperate efforts.

Overcrowding, lack of playing facilities, bad washing arrangements, no outdoor recreations and no holidays out of Shoreditch are the principal evils. A third of the homes under review have no indoor water supply and nearly 70% have no facilities for baths at all. Nearly half have nothing but a kettle for heating water.

Of the group of 12-year-old children, more than half have not been away for as much as a week during the past year . . . three quarters of the younger children and nearly 70% of the older children share a bed.

Mrs Nellie Neale's little bit of paradise – also in Shaftesbury Street – in 1946. Squeezed in among the boxes and tubs of flowers were thirteen rabbits, eight chickens, six ducks and a hammock.

Children of all ages had only the streets to play in and few played any outdoor games. The review cited some sample cases:

Case One: the yard in which the children of 48 families play is very narrow and littered with refuse from rubbish bins; the rooms are in a ghastly condition, dark, damp and overcrowded.

Case Six: only two rooms, both poorly furnished and in bad repair; all the family sleep in one room except the eldest girl, who uses two chairs in the living room.

Stoke Newington's first municipal housing dated from the early 1920s, but in September 1934 the major housing scheme in Lordship Road was almost complete. On 10 September one local paper commented on what was regarded as the unusual step of holding a competition for the development of the site, which was won by Howes and Jackman. It went on to describe the estate:

The scheme comprises a hundred flats, each having a sitting room, kitchen and bathroom and fuel store, and from one to four bedrooms. These are arranged in four blocks, four storeys high, around a large paved courtyard. There will be grass lawns and trees between the buildings and the surrounding roads.

Elevationally the buildings are treated on traditional lines with multi-coloured brick walls, large sash windows and pantile roofs. The windows are divided into small panes . . . partly to reduce the cost of renewing breakages. Some of the windows are picked out with arched heads and small brick balconies to give additional interest. . . . Most of the tenants will be families who are being displaced by the Council's slum clearance programme. . . .

Major municipal schemes were preceded by Ministry of Health inquiries, at which there were some chances for objections to be raised, though little chance of any scheme being radically altered. In November 1938 the LCC proposed to acquire five areas in Haggerston between the Regent's Canal and Hackney Road. The areas:

. . . were mostly residential, the houses being of the two or three storey terrace type, mainly worn out – and there were some badly congested courts within them. The principal defects which [made] . . . the houses unfit for human habitation included bad internal arrangement, such as lack of through passages, badly placed stairs and low rooms . . . dampness, inadequate . . . washing or sanitary accommodation and general disrepair.

Existing residents would be rehoused in LCC estates in London Fields and Bethnal Green and further away in the Pembury estate in Hackney. As part of the scheme, approved workmen's flats were to be built on the length between Whiston Street and Dove Row, while Moye and Jacobin streets would be closed. Areas south of Audrey Street and west of Boston Street would also be redeveloped, while a strip of land from Dove Row to Audrey Street would be left for the Shoreditch Housing Association, an early example of municipal co-operation with a housing association. There was some concern to keep local residents, many of whom worked locally, within close range of their jobs and some of the objections focused on the displacement of cabinet-making firms, that would remove the employment, matters which the LCC witness did not adequately answer.

A Ministry of Food mobile unit visited Hackney in May 1947. Among their stops was Nisbet House in Homerton. In three days members of the Women's Voluntary Service, who crewed it, distributed 1,164 bottles of orange juice, 27 bottles of cod liver oil, 10 tins of dried milk and 15 packets of vitamin tablets to expectant mothers.

In the event the proposed scheme was halted by the onset of the Second World War, and much of what would have been cleared by the LCC fell victim to the attentions of the Luftwaffe when parts of Haggerston were badly bombed.

After the war new municipal housing went up alongside older and war-damaged property. In October 1954 Stoke Newington Observer *reporter Monica Cole visited Shakespeare Walk. On one side was a modern block of council flats, Shelley House:*

But right next door are two bricked up shells which are the haunt of mice, beetles, spiders and small boys. Though they may lie condemned, the houses adjoining them – all in the same terrace – are apparently considered quite fit for human occupation – not, however, by the tenants.

Cole visited 48-year-old Mrs Nellie Veazey, who lived next to these two bricked-up houses abandoned by the Council eighteen months before.

'We're running alive with [mice and beetles]' said Mrs Veazey 'although I spend half-a-crown a week on every kind of stuff you can think of to keep them down. We've nailed tin to the skirtings, but it doesn't keep them out. Then there's the damp. . . . The brickwork is porous and it just seeps through.'

Despite little rain the wall in the living room was still wet. 'And I've had the electric fire playing on that wall for hours to dry it out', she said.

In the front room, the inside of a new dining room suite was turning green with damp. I trod heavily on the floor and the whole room shook so that a vase of flowers nearly toppled off the piano.

'I think the foundations must have slipped', said Mrs Veazey simply. 'Our home is falling to pieces.' This appeared to be almost an understatement. For when I trod on a loose board on the top storey, I fell through the floor. 'We daren't use these rooms at all', said Mrs Veazey.

Picking my way carefully past a hole in the stairs, I descended to a bedroom which could be used – provided that the bed was kept dead in the centre of the room away from the running wall. 'Have you a bathroom?' 'Don't be funny,' said Mrs Veazey, 'we haven't even got a decent sink' and she showed me the dank bare brick scullery and outside lavatory. . . .

'Pull them down? Of course they should', said a despairing housewife further down the road. 'But they've been saying that for years!'

However, concerns about the rents of new Council property remained. In February 1957 the Hackney Gazette *reported that Stoke Newington's Mayor and other civic worthies were booed by Council tenants when they arrived to open new flats and the library on Howard Road. A rent rise was in prospect and the Joint Committee of Tenants and Residents of Stoke Newington used the slogan 'more rent means less food' to highlight the concerns of those who had already had to wait a long time for a new home.*

In Hackney Wick in July 1957 the plans for compulsory purchase of houses in Chapman Road, Daintry Street, Osborne Road, Felsted Street and Prince Edward Road had been announced about a year before and residents and local shopkeepers had been living with the uncertainty of not knowing when their homes would be taken over. Mrs Doreen Reeves of 40 Trowbridge Road had just received a notice to quit in two weeks' time. She lived with her husband and four children in a house where the rain had come in and soaked a meal she was cooking. There were additional worries for some:

Will they be able to afford the rent of a new LCC accommodation when they are re-housed? Most of the people in those parts have been there for years and pay a low rent. Mrs Reeves pays 14s a week. But the people a higher rent could hit are people like Mrs Edie Popperwell, whose two bedroom home at 13 Trowbridge-road only cost her 13s 6d a week rent. 'I don't know where they will send me', she said. 'I would like to stop around here. My son lives near and I have to have someone to go to when I'm ill.' How will she, a widow, pay a higher rent, 'I shall have to go to the National Assistance Board', she said.

In Hackney in 1957 newly weds were evicted from their in-laws' flats so that the latter could be re-housed in smaller flats to enable larger families to move in, provoking a protest by and on behalf of over 800 couples in May. In the same month the Hackney Gazette *reported on the newly opened Tower Court, Clapton Common, a nine-storey block of flats named after an adjoining observation tower said to have been put up eighty years before. One tenant, William Kilbey, who had seen the inside of many Park Lane flats in his job as a french polisher, felt that he had acquired a luxury flat at a non-luxury rent. The scheme provided 67 dwellings for 238 people. The very positive reaction of those who moved into the new tower block was evident, so that the Mayor was able to say 'We can only build dwellings – it is up to the tenants to convert them into real homes', secure in the confidence that they would do just that.*

Not everyone accepted that the housing scheduled to be demolished was beyond repair. At an enquiry into a Homerton development in November 1957, Mrs M.W. Hill, who lived on the edge of the proposed development in Hassett Road, could stand it no longer and, as the Hackney Gazette *for 6 November reported, shouted out:*

'I'm fed up with all this clap-trap. It's moneybags, moneybags all the time. A man here's put his savings into a house and now he's robbed of everything he's got. You don't have any consideration for working people. . . . I want to know why perfectly good houses are being pulled down,' she declared. 'Good homes are being smashed up. There's no sense in it.'

Mrs Hill had been protesting on behalf of a man who had bought a house after checking with the LCC, who had told him there would be no development for between five and ten years.

By 1970 attitudes to older property had begun to change. The Hackney Gazette *carried a report on 6 October 1970 on the rehabilitation of 108 De Beauvoir Road, which had been converted by the De Beauvoir Trust into a one-bedroom and a three-bedroom flat. Opened by a party that included the MP Paul Channon, Joint Parliamentary Secretary to the Minister of Housing and Local Government, Stanley Clinton Davis, the local MP, and the Mayor and Mayoress of Hackney, the £10,000 project had come about through partnership between the Greater London Council, a firm of manufacturers and the housing association. But Hackney Council was still pursuing a policy of demolishing older property. The* Hackney Gazette *carried this report on 5 May 1970:*

18TH CENTURY TERRACE MUST GO
Hackney Housing Committee's abandonment of plans to retain an 18th century terrace on Stoke Newington common was called a 'scandalous decision' at last Wednesday's meeting. Mr [Jack] Youngmark, a physics teacher who has devoted much of his time and money to renovating one of the houses in Sanford-terrace, alleged 'Every effort has been made by the Council to discourage people from getting on with improvements. They are far more interested in compelling existing owners to sell out at consequently lowered prices.'

Sanford Terrace, 1970.

The 13 houses in the terrace are on the Ministry of Housing's list of buildings of historical or architectural interest. They were built by a family called Sanford in 1788.

A few months ago, after deliberating the subject for over a year, the Committee decided by the casting vote of the chairman, Councillor David Henderson, to retain the terrace in the proposed Smalley-road redevelopment scheme. But it was hoped that the buildings would be smartened up – and that possibly a Housing Association might take on the job.

But by an overwhelming majority the Committee decided in favour of demolition of all but Mr Youngmark's house. This was because no Housing Associations had come forward with any plans and because it was felt that apart from Mr Youngmark, no owner had shown interest in improving their properties.

Henderson claimed he was disappointed in the owners' response – although three of the terrace were owned by the Council itself. Jack Youngmark, a member of the Hackney Society and the Society for the Protection of Ancient Buildings (SPAB), was able to claim his house, bought in December 1965, also now included a self-contained flat and the whole had cost the same as a two-bedroom council flat and a double garage.

By October 1970, the Council's demolition decision had been reversed, but the Council still intended to compulsorily purchase 9–20 in the terrace, with a view to converting them to flats. However, the main frontage was to be restored and any interior mouldings and other features identified by the GLC Historic Buildings section would be retained. Opponents of the compulsory purchase order included the Hackney Society, the Georgian Group and SPAB; the Hackney Society still favoured renovation by resident owners.

Government restrictions on council expenditure blocked Hackney Council repairing properties it owned and in February 1981 it put up 'wanted' posters, featuring the head of the relevant minister, Michael Heseltine, which were then attached to the empty houses. Nor did Hackney welcome government legislation that gave Council tenants the right to buy their own houses. The Hackney Gazette *of 3 October 1980 reported that the Council intended to proceed slowly and that the Broad Left Group on the Council were wholly opposed and would not help any tenant who approached them. Only one sale went through in February 1981, when the Council sold a roofless property in Ufton Grove it had previously bought for £1 through an estate agent for £8,250 – but only because the Council could not afford repairs. However, money was made available to housing associations. This report came from the* Hackney Gazette *of 7 December 1982:*

FAMILIES OCCUPY HISTORIC HOMES
Hoxton's unique row of early 19th century houses, renovated at a cost of £1.5 million, were formally opened on Friday.

Shepherdess Walk was built in 1830 when Kingsland Waste was open fields and Hackney was a pleasant suburban village. At that time Hoxton was a new town – a sort of premature Milton Keynes. The houses were still occupied in the 1970s but they had declined so badly that the council was planning to knock them down.

Then they became listed as buildings of architectural and historical importance and the Circle 33 Housing Association took on the job of upgrading them into the 20th century. With grants from the Department of the Environment, the GLC and

Hackney Council, the buildings were gutted and almost completely rebuilt. The facades were left intact but inside the open hearths were replaced by gas fires and central heating.

At a cost of £37,500 each for forty houses the housing association felt they had not overspent in preserving and converting the houses, although one tenant found that one house had a condensation problem.

With considerable empty Council property and many people looking for somewhere to live, squatting seemed the logical conclusion. Local squatters were mobilized as early as 1970 when the Hackney Squatting Organization joined with the Duncan House Tenants Association and members of Homes for the Homeless to disrupt a Hackney Council meeting, as reported in the Hackney Gazette *on 17 April of that year. Not all local people agreed with their councillors however. This report comes from the* Hackney Gazette *of 11 January 1983:*

NEIGHBOURS' PLEA FOR SQUATTERS FALLS ON DEAF EARS
Most people believe squatters lower the tone of the neighbourhood and would be better evicted by the council.

But residents in Marlborough Avenue, just off London Fields, like their squatters so much that they are petitioning the council to let them stay. Massimo Pezzati and Brigitte Gohides moved into a derelict house on the street last August. They spent months painting and decorating their house, put in a new heater, repaired the plumbing and replaced window panes. Four people moved into the next-door house a little later and started doing up their house in the same way.

But in December they received eviction notices . . . from Hackney Council . . . and the GLC because the two councils were going to start doing up their properties. Then neighbours Stuart Goodman and Penny Thomas sent a letter to the council on behalf of Massimo Pezzati and Brigitte Gohides. 'They are very nice people and they have done a lot for the community. It is especially good for us because, when the house was empty, we had several attempted break-ins and the place was damp on that side' said Mr Goodman.

Now a petition asking that the squatters be given short life housing status has been signed by 13 residents and sent to the council. The council are sympathetic but unbending. 'The property is one of a

The Marlborough Avenue squatters, 1983.

number in the Broadway market area that is due for renovation and that is why we have to evict them. Work on the houses is due to start in the spring' said a council spokesman.

HEALTH AND WORKHOUSES

Before 1930 both Hackney and St Leonard's hospitals were workhouses, though both included infirmaries for the care of the sick. In June 1872 a Hackney Gazette *reporter visited both establishments and, in a style distinctly influenced by Dickens, provided two long pieces for his paper. At Hackney the 'good, comfortable and portly' Mr and Mrs Johnson, the Master and Mistress, were his guides. From the window of their reception room he could see:*

. . . the general plan of the main buildings, which constitute three sides of an oblong square, the right wing being devoted to female inhabitants and the left to the male. Each wing is three storeys high and is . . . composed of a series of houses, each having a flight of stone stairs leading from the outside to the uppermost rooms. The two wings are separated by a high wall which is now draped with the lovely foliage of many beautiful trees.

Passing the gardens, the new block with the Board of Guardians offices, greenhouses and a corner with pigs, the reporter was taken into the basement. On route was the Old Women's Dining Hall:

. . . with double rows of 'desks' rather than tables . . . ranged in lines with a passage in between them. At the end is a raised platform with a table from which the dinners are supplied and upon it were whole battalions of clean white mugs, each bearing the useful piece of information that it belongs to the parish.

Beyond lay the Cookery with its five steam boilers, the Old Men's Dining Rooms and a range of stores, before the reporter was taken through the women's side of the house:

The first of course is the 'Receiving Room' and adjacent . . . the place where they are 'bath'd' and their clothing changed; that which they were previously wearing being taken to the fumigation room . . . And subsequently placed aside for personal use should the women again leave the Workhouse. . . .

Then we came to the 'Aged Ward' where about forty poor old creatures uniformly dressed and "'clean as a new pin' were busily plying the needle, for all that description of work, even to the making of dresses, is performed in the house. There was a bright fire burning and an air of cheerfulness and comfort, far different from that which 'outsiders' have been led to believe. As we entered they all rose, but upon being kindly spoken to by the Matron, for whom they evidently entertained a high respect, they seated themselves and resumed the work on which they were engaged.

In the sick rooms there were nurses in attendance and every room had high-backed and padded chairs beside the beds.

. . . tea was being made in little pots. However strict order was kept through the house, and silence everywhere except the room for new mothers and presumably the

The Women's Ward, Hackney Union Workhouse, *c.* 1900.

laundry room, where able bodied women washed, ironed, and used the mangles. The men, if not working in the house, had to pick 4lbs of oakum a day or break up eight bushels of stones.

At Shoreditch the older children were sent to complete their education at Union schools at Brentwoood in Essex. After 1876 management of the schools passed to Hackney. By the 1890s many of the children sent out there came from the poorest part of the borough, Hackney Wick, and it was here that was most affected when a case of cruelty by Ella Gillespie, an infants' nurse, came to light in 1894. In evidence reported to the Board of Guardians by the School Committee and which appeared in the Hackney Gazette *for 20 April 1894 the first details were made public:*

. . . it appeared that many of the children had been dragged out of bed and subjected to what is known as 'basket drill', that is they had to walk about the room for a long time with baskets containing their clothes on their heads, and if any article was dropped they were severely thrashed. Children had had their toes bruised by strokes from a cane; others again had had their heads bruised through being knocked against the wall. The reason the children gave for not complaining was because they were afraid of the nurse.

It was later revealed that Gillespie had also whipped children on their naked bodies with stinging nettles, cut a child's head with a bunch of keys, made children kneel on wire guards surrounding hot water pipes, immersed children's heads in buckets of water and continually beaten them on the hands and feet. In the end the basket drill was stopped when another nurse threatened to report it if she saw it again. Girls who had left the school and were working as domestic servants had corroborated the evidence of the children.

Youngsters participating in the annual sports day at the Brentwood Poor Law School, 1898.

. . . One of the worst features in the case was that relating to water. The children in the hot summer months were afraid to ask the nurse for water as they knew it meant another thrashing and were driven by the pangs of thirst to go to the w.c, and dip the water out of the pans with their hands and drink it. That such a state of things could have gone on for eleven years and not be discovered by the officials was almost incredible.

One child, Eliza Clarke, admitted in April 1893, was treated, apparently successfully, for ophthalmia and an ulcer of the anus, but was back in the infirmary in December with a swelling on her head which proved to be a fatal abscess. The child had also been ill-treated by Gillespie, though medical opinion could not directly prove she had been responsible for the illness. But her other cruel behaviour was enough for the Guardians to have her successfully prosecuted and to institute a thorough shake up of the management of Brentwood schools.

Hoxton had a long association with the treatment of the mentally ill. One of the oldest of the private lunatic asylums was Hoxton House on the east side of the street, founded in 1695. A journalist visited the establishment in May 1885 and was shown around by the resident medical superintendent, Dr J.F. Woods:

It is a large and somewhat straggling block of buildings to the side of the footway. Nowadays its situation cannot be considered salubrious . . . but once within its walls one would have no cause to know it was placed in one of the most densely populous of the neighbourhoods of the east.

The exterior of Brentwood Poor Law School, *c.* 1898. It was built for the benefit of Shoreditch children in 1854.

It was Sunday morning when the writer . . . visited the Asylum. In Hoxton-street most of the shops were open, costermongers' barrows plentiful and a good deal of commerce being transacted amongst such commodities as fish, vegetables, live birds and rats, dogs and rabbits, old clothes, cast-off boots, ice cream and rusty pieces of old iron.

Woods took the reporter through a garden with circling paths and flowerbeds, which was available to the patients. There were walls, but Woods claimed he was lowering them:

'I want to get rid, as far as possible, of all semblance of gloom and confinement'.

They passed on into a recreation room for female patients, where the women were seated down each side of

. . . an immense room, with tables down the centre and lofty windows throughout the extent of one side. The walls are tinted lively salmons, red and pinks. . . . [T]heir stiffness is broken by the 'picture-rail' border fringe and an effective dado. The ceiling too is papered with delicately harmonised tints and stencilled with graceful designs, while pictures, plaques, and vases of lively colours are displayed in all the artistic nooks and crannies. The floor is of polished oak, the fireplace is tiled in the latest style of decorative art, and even the door panels have been removed for Perry's 'glacial' design in imitation of stained glass to be substituted. Nothing could be more cheerful and enlivening than the general effect, or more calculated, we would imagine, to dispel the melancholia that is one of the chief causes of insanity.

Patients included those suffering from memory loss and delusions. Woods was also at pains to point out his high success rate of cured cases. There were additional staircases to the dormitories to serve as escape routes in case of fire, and electric bells in all parts of the building.

. . . Three hundred inmates were recently entertained with a fancy dress ball, when the gardens were illuminated and everything done to make the affair a thorough and pleasant diversion, while concerts and dances are frequent during the winter months, and picnics, drives and visits to places of public entertainment, under due supervision, provided during the summer.

Woods' hospitality evidently produced the article he had hoped for – but the contrast with the kind of conditions that had prevailed sixty years before in private asylums was striking. Hoxton House was closed in 1902, and the red-brick house still bearing that name in Hoxton Street is the last physical part of the asylum to survive.

Smallpox was a regular threat to the community. This report comes from a local paper of 3 January 1902.

SMALLPOX AT HACKNEY AND STOKE NEWINGTON
Considerable alarm has been occasioned by the report of a serious recurrence of smallpox in Hackney and Stoke Newington. . . . The disease . . . probably originated with a family of costermongers in High Street, Stoke Newington, and has been most prevalent in the narrow courts on either side of that thoroughfare. The first victim was Mrs Warby of Sanford-lane – the filthy condition of which place was remarked upon at the meeting of the Hackney Board of Guardians on Wednesday, when it was reported that twenty-one cases of smallpox had been removed from the districts of Hackney and Stoke Newington in fourteen days.

Mrs Warby's illness had originally been diagnosed as blood poisoning, until Hackney's Medical Officer of Health recognised it as smallpox, by which time it was too late for Mrs Warby, who died before she could be removed by ambulance.

Some forty persons had, it appeared, come into contact with the deceased, most of them belonging to the costermonger class. . . . By joint and immediate action on the part of the medical officers of [Hackney, Stoke Newington and Islington] close observation was kept on these persons and up to Tuesday afternoon seventeen of them . . . had been stricken with the disease. As a result of the outbreak the surgeries of many of the local doctors have been literally inundated with subjects for vaccination, whilst numbers of people in the habit of purchasing goods at the costermongers' stalls have now withheld their custom and destroyed any purchases they have made. . . . Yesterday's returns showed that 24 fresh cases of smallpox had occurred in different parts of the Metropolis during the day, including six in Hackney.

A hazard of a different kind was caused by the great smog of the winter of 1952. Londoners were used to 'pea-soupers', but weather conditions made this one especially severe. This report comes from the Hackney Gazette *of 10 December 1952.*

FOUR DAYS' FOG: DEATH AND CHAOS
Motor Cyclist killed in collision with Bus. Man found dead on railway lines.

Four days' fog, which blanketed Greater London from Friday to Monday, was particularly severe in North-east London, where deaths were caused, crime had a little hey-day and transport, when not completely immobilised, was reduced to a cautious crawl. It was the worst fog within local memory.

The accidents included a fatality when a motorcycle combination collided with a trolleybus in Kingsland High Street, an elderly man of German descent found dead on the railway lines at Stoke Newington, an elderly woman who walked off the towpath and into the Lea (and was rescued) and an unfortunate dog walker who tripped over the animal's lead and fractured his knee cap.

Although the fog cleared away from many areas in London on Monday, a breeze blew it eastwards to the Lea Valley, where it stayed to increase the chaotic conditions in Clapton, Homerton and large areas of Shoreditch and Bethnal Green.

Conditions in Kingsland-road between Dalston Junction and Shoreditch Church as people groped their way home from work or shopping on Monday evening were like a bad dream, with lorries, buses and cars edging their way perilously. Many wandered on to the wrong side of the road and added to the nearly desperate confusion.

A number of Gazette staff, who were walking with three other persons towards Shoreditch, had a close escape when a heavy lorry suddenly charged up on the pavement at the corner of Laburnum-street and stopped within inches of the little party as they yelled in alarm. Many people, unable to get home by bus, invaded Old-street Tube Station where there were long queues and crowded platforms.

Waiting times for hospital beds is not a new issue. This report is from the Hackney Gazette *of 24 May 1948, two months before the introduction of the National Health Service.*

PATIENTS WAITING FOR HOSPITAL BEDS. RISK OF DISEASE SPREADING
After hearing an address by Dr C.K. Cullen, Tuberculosis Officer for Shoreditch at the Hackney Labour Exchange on Thursday evening, with reference to the acute staffing position in hospitals, the Hackney Trades council decided to form a committee to consider methods of speeding up the recruitment of nurses.

Dr Cullen said the situation with regard to tuberculosis patients was particularly serious. Anything from nine months to a year was the normal waiting period for a hospital bed. This meant that treatment which might have been successful in the early stages might no longer be effective, and the outcome was sometimes the death of the patient.

It was impossible to give people proper care and attention in overcrowded conditions in their homes and there was a risk of spreading the disease. The position was often as bad with other patients. Quite recently a person with a particular heart condition had tried to get into St Leonard's Hospital and was told that the nearest vacancy was at Northwood in Middlesex.

The trouble in East London was the shortage of nurses, and in West London it was the lack of domestic staff. Hackney Hospital had 200 beds empty through inadequate nursing staff.

Dr Cullen also felt that working conditions for nurses needed to be improved and that tyrannical practices by matrons, combined with petty restrictions in force in many hospitals, were a further barrier to recruitment. Also:

They should not go around looking for any particular type of girl. The ordinary girls who had manned the first-aid posts during the war would make admirable nurses.

Guests at a dance held at St Leonard's Hospital, January 1963.

Hackney Council debated another health issue in January 1958, when Councillor Arthur Super advocated putting notices on lampposts warning people of the danger of smoking and lung cancer. This was against a total of local deaths from lung cancer and bronchitus that had risen from forty-nine in 1946 to eighty-four in 1956.

'There is no doubt that if the public were alive to the danger, they could take preventative action' urged Councillor Super. Stressing the need to educate people – especially the young – on the danger of smoking, he said there were some who said that there was a lot of fuss being made about nothing.

By 1964 drug-taking was beginning to be a problem and Dr Daphne Sasieni of the Central Council for Health Education addressed a conference of youth leaders at Shoreditch Town Hall on purple-heart pills and their effects on teenagers. This report comes from the Hackney Gazette *of 17 April 1964.*

PURPLE HEART PROBLEM DOES EXIST
Teenagers taking purple heart pills should be made to realize that there are only 24 hours in a day. 'Six or eight of them have to be spent sleeping and, no matter what you take, the account has to be settled in the end', stated Dr Sasieni.

After discussion the youth leaders agreed there was a problem. Dr Sasieni thought that the cases might have been exaggerated but Robin Griffin, leader of the Explorers' Club at Shoreditch School, disagreed:

Mr Griffin said that children from the school had appeared on a television programme transmitted from a Dalston dance hall and admitted taking the drug. 'There does seem to be some ground for being worried about it' he said, adding that boys from the school, when told recently about a seven-miles walk, said 'All right, we

Dr Daphne Sasieni at the Shoreditch Town Hall conference on drug-taking, 1964.

will need these' and popped some pep-pills in their mouths. 'They told me they didn't have an adverse effect' said Mr Griffin.

Discussion ranged over the dangers of addiction, supply through clubs by pushers and the indiscriminate use of a wide range of tablets by adults. Griffin added that he had talked to teenagers about the issue and felt that taking purple hearts might be slowly going out of fashion, though he understood they took the pills to give them energy for night parties.

The Revd Kenneth Loveless, Rural Dean of Shoreditch, asked why they needed artificial stimulants. He didn't need them when, as a young man, he stayed up all night doing the Charleston.

The delegate from the Ministry of Education concluded the conference by claiming that a forthcoming parliamentary bill would make these drugs harder to obtain and hoping that the fashion for taking them would die a natural death.

From the mid-1970s there were plans to rationalize local hospitals by closing some and make others specialize in particular areas. In July 1975 petitions were circulating concerning proposals to close the Metropolitan Hospital, turn the German into a geriatric hospital and the Mothers, then Hackney's principal maternity hospital, into one for people with mental handicaps (in the terminology of the time). The only good news was a reprieve for Britain's single Jewish maternity hospital, the Bearsted Memorial Hospital at Stoke Newington. Despite a local petition, Health Minister Barbara Castle refused to intervene and in November it was confirmed that the closure of the Metropolitan and Eastern

The Metropolitan Hospital, Kingsland Road, 1921.

hospitals would go ahead. By December of the same year a mini-hospital was announced for the site of the closed Eastern Hospital. But this was not the end of the closures. This report comes from the Hackney Gazette *for 22 October 1982.*

FOUR LOCAL HOSPITALS MAY CLOSE

Hackney's health chiefs plan to axe four local hospitals in the 1980s – and argue that the move will lead to a better health service.

Facing the chop are St Leonard's in Shoreditch, the German in Dalston, St Matthew's in Hoxton and the Mothers' in Lower Clapton. Treatment currently available at the four will in future be given at bigger and better hospitals – Barts in the City and a brand new Homerton Hospital now being built, they say.

The proposals are outlined in the City and Hackney Health Authority's draft plan for 1983–86 now being discussed. It is planned to shut down the German, St Matthew's and the Mother's towards the end of the decade, but St Leonard's could go as early as 1984.

The Hackney Community Health Council was concerned about St Leonard's, whose closure before the opening of the new Homerton hospital would lead to serious cuts in service, especially with the projected cuts of £19.5m outlined in the draft plan. In the event, all four hospitals did close and it took longer than originally planned before Homerton Hospital reached its initial projected capacity. Hackney was also affected by the loss of accident and emergency services at St Bartholomew's Hospital in the 1990s.

CHAPTER FIVE

LOCAL GOVERNMENT, SCHOOLS AND TRANSPORT

LOCAL GOVERNMENT

One aspect of the governance of the locality that is centrally organized is the census of population, which has taken place every ten years since 1801 (with the exception of 1941). This account by a former enumerator for the 1871 census appeared in the Hackney & Kingsland Gazette *for 8 April 1871.*

. . . A great deal had been done to make people understand the Census papers. Many of the people I've been to seemed to enjoy the importance of filling in a return. It was a novelty to some of them to find anyone who cared whether they were married or single, or where they were born, or what they did. Assured that the Government . . . meant them no harm, they jumped with fatal facility to the opposite conclusion and assumed that the authorities were about to interfere actively for their good. The Census paper was a talisman which, if the proper words were inserted in the proper place and at the proper time, would bring good luck; and each dweller in a court or alley made it his or her business to bring to light all omissions or inaccuracies on the part of their neighbours. I saw what was passing in many a simple mind, and I felt like an imposter when I took some papers back, and heard of the hopes they had roused. It is the ladies . . . and the would be gentilities who have bothered me most and who have seemed the most obstructive. Take cooks for example. I don't know whether there is anything in the practice of roasting and boiling which induces people to mendacity, but in the course of my rounds the cooks have been more perverse than any of their fellows. They all made themselves so absurdly young, and in the few instances in which I hesitated a doubt as to whether a palpable forty year-older was justified in describing herself as twenty seven, the barefaced way in which the effect of a kitchen fire on a complexion and the consequent 'ageing' of the appearance were put forward was quite staggering. . . . I met other odd people whose peculiarities were, as I thought, remarkable. There was one old lady, who would tell me stories of the sad cases of destitution she had known of, and which had arisen from the head of a family signing his name incautiously at the request of someone else. I had the greatest difficulty in persuading her that a census paper is not a bill of exchange. . . . There was the pragmatical little man, too, who lodged over the butcher's shop and who insisted on describing himself as 'gentleman' in spite of that vague phrase having been expressly forbidden in the printed directions. He was a retired haberdasher and he did not like to say so; while the shopmen would call themselves 'assistants'; the people who boggled over trifles and who could not be made to understand either the responsibility of a written statement or the value of my time – all these belonged to the half-educated classes. The two extremes of society performed their part towards the Census office cheerfully and satisfactorily, and the shortcomings (which after all have been very inconsiderable) all arose among those who were uncertain as to their social position and feared to write themselves down in the world. As a means of seeing household interiors and of becoming acquainted with a thousand and one particulars of the inner life of the members of the community in which you live, there is, believe me, nothing to approach the act of going the Census rounds.

St Leonard's Vicarage, Hoxton Square. Watercolour by Thomas Shepherd, *c.* 1844.

Parish government was replaced by vestries or local boards in inner London in 1856. Shoreditch's new vestry had 120 members and also had to find somewhere to conduct their business. An 'Old Shoreditch Observer' produced a series of reminiscence pieces in the Hackney Express & Shoreditch Observer, *of which this formed part of an article in the issue of 12 March 1898, recalling the period before the new Town Hall was finished:*

Delay was a serious matter in the carrying on of parochial business, seeing that the offices of the Vestry were at the old Vicarage in Hoxton-square, placed at the disposal of the new vestry by the late Rev Simpson Evans, who lived at Stoke Newington. The building afforded most excellent makeshift offices; but the Vestry's place of meeting was at the schoolroom of the New Tabernacle in Old-street-road, which had to be fitted up for each meeting by the parish labourers with platform, tables, seats etc and all the books, papers, pens and ink were taken over from the offices in wheelbarrows from Hoxton-square and removed back again to the offices after the vestry was over. The place was so small that if all the Vestrymen had attended there would have been not nearly room enough and no room for the indignant rate-payers.

Nor was the Town Hall quite as well built as it ought to have been. This report appeared in the Hackney & Kingsland Gazette *of 18 September 1869.*

Our Shoreditch neighbours seem to be very unfortunate with their Town Hall; scarcely a week passes over, but we hear of something in connection with it – the other day the walls were not strong enough to support the roof and were visibly bulging out, then the staircases were called into question and now we are told that there is considerable danger that . . . the place will burn down. We are told that the heat arising from the gas pipes had caused the wood-work of the ceiling to become so hot that the thermometer had registered it at 200 degrees [Fahrenheit] and it was even above that but the thermometer 'could not further go'. We hear that the pipes are only six inches from the ceiling while . . . they shall in no case be less than fourteen inches.

The author of the piece suggested that alterations be made to save the building from the disaster many predicted. In the event there was no fire until 1904, when the main meeting room and the roof were destroyed in a fierce blaze.

Shoreditch Town Hall when it was first built, 1867.

Shoreditch Vestry planned and implemented some major municipal programmes from the late 1880s, including the enlargement of the original library in Kingsland Road, completed in 1886 and the implementation of a new library, baths and an electricity generating station (which generated power from burning rubbish) on Pitfield Street, completed in 1899. However, just before the vestry was set to be replaced by a Borough Council in 1901, the cost of this and of the pioneering community housing work in the Provost Street area left a deficit for the new Borough Council to try to close. Rates were also a trying business for Hackney's new council and in April 1902 an all night sitting that lasted eight hours failed to arrive at a decision. Our 'Local Longer' in the Hackney Gazette *commented on the spirit of construction that prevailed:*

Time is wasted and public money squandered by members whose main desire appeared to be to use the Council Chamber for anything but the proper purpose for which it is intended. The personalities that were freely indulged in at Monday's meeting would not make very edifying reading, while to say that some of the epithets bandied about were unparliamentary is to but very mildly state the case. All this may have been very entertaining to the gallery, but the matter is too serious to be lightly passed over.

While there is an evident desire on the part of some members to facilitate public work and to restore order out of the present muddled state of our parochial business, there is unfortunately a rancorous opposition which renders progress in matters of detail extremely difficult. The present constitution of the borough Council is scarcely an ideal one and it remains for the ratepayers to determine how far this state of things shall be allowed to go. Perhaps a series of meetings in different parts of the Borough would tend to focus public opinion upon a condition of affairs which is far more grave than is generally imagined. . . .

Hackney did have some early municipal successes of its own, principally the initiation of local electricity supply on 31 October 1901. This report comes from the Hackney & Kingsland Gazette *of the previous day:*

The switching on of the electric current at Hackney to-morrow afternoon will mark an interesting epoch in the municipal life of the Borough. It is certainly significant that the Borough Council in the first year of its existence should witness the opening of so huge an undertaking as that represented by the electricity and dust destructor works at Millfield-road. . . . The works themselves are probably the most complete and up-to-date in the Kingdom. They stand on a site of about five acres, which allows for ample means of extension, and have the advantage of a frontage to the River Lea, [for] the supply of fuel and the shipment of clinker. . . . For the purposes

Hackney Electricity Generating Station, viewed from the River Lea, 1939.

of street lighting, three hundred and twenty arc lamps are to be employed, placed at distances of from fifty to sixty feet apart, and the posts have been designed so that the top of each lamp is about twenty one feet from the ground. In respect of private lighting, a system of free wiring has been arranged by which consumers may have wires and lamps fitted . . . on the quarterly payment of 5½d per lamp. Any person, however, has the option of having his house wired at his own expense and thus save these charges or he may, under certain circumstances, purchase the whole of the wires and fittings from the 'free wiring' company. . . . [I]f the undertaking is to be the great success hoped for, however, no stone should be left unturned to make consumption of the current as universal as possible and if wisdom and tact are exercised in the work we may still hope to see the large initial expense of the scheme recouped.

Hackney's works passed to the nationalized electricity industry in 1948. The London division of the Central Electricity Authority brought coal into London for its power stations on its own boats – and for a period in the 1950s, there was a 2,700-ton steam-powered boat rejoicing in the title SS Hackney *bringing coal from South Wales or the north-east.*

Hackney had provided municipal laundries as early as 1934, but in 1958 a service was introduced for all Hackney people, when a laundrette opened in Old Street, Stamford Hill. With twenty washing machines and six spin driers, the new venture was run by Hackney's Baths Department, who publicized the opening with 4,000 printed balloons. Hackney's baths superintendent for many years was L.F. James. The Hackney Gazette *reported on another innovatory service on 2 February 1962.*

TAKING AN 'AEROTONE' IN HACKNEY

Hackney Baths, Lower Clapton Road, *c.* 1966.

For an aerotone, go to Hackney. At central bath in Lower Clapton-road, is the only local authority aerotone bath north of the Thames. Athletes use it to tone up strained muscles, so do bruised footballers, so do people with various forms of rheumatism, people with low blood pressure, high blood pressure, poor circulation, strains and varicose veins. It is aid to relieve mental depression, and if you have none of these complaints, it will tone you up, make you feel on top of the world.

James had installed the aerotone bath nine years before. He was already aware of the beneficial effects of hot water for rheumatism and got the chance to try the aerotone bath for himself when he visited the inventor, Professor Oliver, at

Edinburgh University. When it was installed at Hackney, the only two others in London were at Bermondsey and Lambeth.

The aerotone bath provides an all-over massage by forcing air at considerable pressure through water. This does what no masseuse can do, it applies gentle, non-stop massage and warmth, the water being kept at a temperature of between 94 and 100 F. The Hackney aerotone bath is a stainless steel cylinder about six feet deep and half sunk in the floor. The bather descends by steps into the bubbling water and sits on a stainless steel stool with water up to the neck. An operator regulates the heat of the water and the pressure at which the air is forced through holes in the bottom of the cylinder.

Treatment usually lasted for 20 minutes. Injured footballers formed regular customers – including members of the Leyton Orient, Arsenal and Tottenham teams, and the oldest customer was eighty. The bath cost 3s 6d and James was hoping to replace one of his slipper baths with another machine.

The London Borough of Hackney came into being on 1 April 1965. But it could have all been different. The Hackney Gazette *of 26 July 1963 reported on the debate when the Advisory Committee on the re-organization failed to agree on a name:*

Stoke Newington's representatives, it seems, had favoured Amherst or Kingsland, while the Shoreditch delegation plumped for Kingsland. Rather strangely, Kingsland does not appear to have appealed to the Hackney representatives at all, and on their advice, the Council has now decided to inform . . . the Minister of Housing and Local Government, that Dalston would be more appropriate than any other designation . . .

The matter was not resolved at that stage, and in the end 'Hackney' was proposed, though both Shoreditch and Stoke Newington supported 'Kingsland' instead. Councillor David Gold could have been more tactful when he urged Stoke Newington councillors to accept the Minister's decision in January 1964:

'. . . and settle down to thinking that way. Hackney is the greater borough.'

A remark that brought members to their feet shouting their grievances. As Councillor H.J. Lobenstein put it:

'If the name of this borough is going to be Hackney and the administration of this borough is going to be in Hackney, then this is going to be a take over by Hackney. The smaller partners will be swallowed up. Stoke Newington has a history and wants to preserve something of its identity.'

The issue of the locality of control in the new London borough was a theme that was to surface again. In 1975 Shoreditch residents fought and won a campaign to stop the closure of Shoreditch Town Hall and were eventually successful in retaining it for direct use by the local authority for another twenty years. And in November 1982 the Hackney Gazette *reported on the 'Hackney Goes Local' initiative, in which it was proposed to create thirty mini town halls around the borough to bring the delivery of services closer to people. Costed at between £2 million and £13 million, the scheme, one of a number of initiatives by a new group of Labour councillors elected in 1982, laid the foundations for the later neighbourhood offices, though one of its slogans – 'we aim to make local government a joy'*

– was a little optimistic. In the end battles with central government over rates and funding prevented the plan being fully implemented, but the issues of accountability at neighbourhood level remained.

Today loud music is one of the problems raised with local councils. But it was also an issue in the nineteenth century, and then there was nothing for it but a letter to the Editor. This piece is from the Hackney Gazette *of 28 August 1869:*

AN ORGANIC NUISANCE

Sir – We have frequently heard of Mr Babbage and the Organ nuisance, but I question whether the great mathematician ever experienced such an annoyance and nuisance as the one now complained of, viz a powerful organ in the Iron Chapel, Milton-road, sending forth dismal and doleful tones at the early morning hour of 6 and continuing until 8. These unearthly, rumbling grumbling attacks on the slumber of the neighbourhood occur nearly every morning. The direful noses being most unmistakeably produced by the efforts of amateurs or learners, surely they ought to find some other place than a chapel for amateur practice or at all events they might evince a little more discretion and consideration in selection of the time for their noisy and anti-musical infliction. Hoping publicity may abate the annoyance complained, I am, Sir, one tired of

Organ Jargon.

The development of Hackney put more pressure on Hackney Marshes and the River Lea, as industrial and housing demands reduced the potential of both for recreation. In 1935 30 acres of Hackney Marsh were lost, despite substantial local opposition, when the land was taken by the LCC to build the Kingsmead estate. Pollution of the River Lea from sewage was a perennial problem from the mid-nineteenth century and remained so into the early 1960s. This report comes from the Stoke Newington Observer *of 16 June 1961:*

RIVER LEA IS AN OPEN SEWER

The Mayor of Hackney (Ald. Louis Sherman) is planning a campaign to clean up the River Lea. He is appalled by the filth which is pumped into the river every day and would like the authorities responsible for keeping the river clean to 'use the powers which parliament provided to do so'.

Sherman envisaged the Lea becoming 'another South Bank':

He envisages a promenade lined by a boulevard of trees, a paved area with facilities for refreshment, music and other recreational amenities which 'East Londoners so badly need'.

Dozens of people who live in boats along banks of the Lea at Spring Hill are feeling bitter about the large quantities of oil and tar pumped into the river, which, they say are 'ruining the timbers of our vessels'. Mrs Ann Fox, who lives aboard *Icot*, a converted landing craft, with her husband John and their 18-month-old baby, described the river as 'an open sewer'. She added that no animal life could exist in the lower reaches of the river.

'A few weeks ago the surface was a mass of dead fish. A little later several swans almost sank, because their [feathers] were covered with oil and tar . . .'

Radley's boatyard, Springfield Park, 1969.

The river dwellers blamed Middlesex County Council for discharging raw sewage, though a spokesman for the Council denied this and even claimed that he had drunk the water himself, and that the solid sewage was sold off as manure. But periodically the pollution reached dangerous heights:

Mr R.A. Tyrell, who hires out rowing boats, said that several weeks ago it was impossible to let any boats out on the river. 'There was at least an inch of thick black oil and tar on the surface. I had to take all my boats out and it took me days to get them clean. If a boy falls into the river he has to be taken to hospital for injections. Not because he is suffering from shock, but because of the great danger of infection.'

The establishment of the Lee Valley Regional Park Authority in 1967 and the closure of some of the industrial plants in the decades that followed did eventually diminish the serious levels of pollution of the early 1960s.

In September 1932 the extension of the Piccadilly Line from Finsbury Park to Arnos Grove was completed. The Hackney Gazette *of 19 September had a mixed reaction. Services would be improved and not be slowed down in fog, while*

So replete are the provisions made for the public safety and convenience that it will be easier to lose one's train than one's life. Even would-be suicides are catered for as there is a large trough at each station for them to fall into!

But Hackney and Stoke Newington had hoped for something different:

. . . in the shape of underground extensions from the City to Tottenham in one direction and Waltham Cross in the other, in addition to the electrification of existing railways, but ultimately the now partially completed scheme was thrust

The bus and tram interchange station at Manor House under construction, 1932.

upon them and was given precedence at the public enquiry which they were mainly instrumental in securing as far back as October 1926. The view of the London electric railways at that time was that the volume of traffic would not be sufficiently great or remunerative to warrant the cost of carrying the Tube from Liverpool Street northwards, and the fact that a railway from Eastcheap to Waltham Cross, with a branch to Leyton, was authorised in 1905 and never proceeded with owing to lack of funds was quoted to the detriment of the project.

Still, the new Tube extension will bring with it many advantages that will not be unreaped by residents in our immediate locality. It was shown at the enquiry that during a normal day only 30% of the whole traffic handled by the Piccadilly Railway at Finsbury park was local and that the remaining 70% came from the outer suburbs. Thus we may look to a great relief of street transport and a corresponding acceleration of bus and tram services going westwards. The interchange station at Manor House for tramway users will be an immense boon, as it will afford direct access from Tube trains to tramcars and vice-versa, and less overcrowding of street conveyances will mean increased comfort and less delay, during rush hours especially.

Bus services to some parts of Hackney were a regular cause of complaint. In April 1950 Kingsmead estate tenants staged a poster parade outside London Transport headquarters at 55 Broadway, Westminster, about poor services. In 1961 it was the space race that prompted an apposite local comparison from Alderman Louis Sherman, as reported in the Hackney Gazette *of 2 May:*

COSMONAUTS AND HACKNEY TRANSPORT
Alderman Louis Sherman criticised London Transport at the monthly meeting of Hackney Council, when commenting on the refusal of the L.T.E. to increase the 253 bus service, or extend the 178 route from Clapton Pond to Manor House.

'It seems amazing that Russia can circle the earth in 87 minutes and yet it can take 45 minutes to come from Manor House to the Town Hall by bus', said Alderman Sherman. The L.T.E. have a duty to supply a transport service, but seem quite unable to run one, he said.

On other occasions, added the Alderman, one went expecting to wait 40 minutes, and then found two or three buses all together. But anyone who missed that 'group' would have to wait a long time for another bus. . . .

In August 1961 the last trolleybus services were run in Hackney. Trolleybuses began to replace trams in the late 1930s and the last part of the Hackney route system ran from Balls Pond Road along parts of Southgate Road to the southern boundary at the junction with De Beauvoir Crescent. The same month also saw the introduction of the first part of the South Hackney one-way system,

'Hop on a bus . . . to Prague'. Councillor George Sylvester and his wife set off on the No. 11 bus for a fortnight's round trip to Czechoslovakia, June 1965.

mostly affecting the eastern end of Well Street, Wick Road and roads east of Well Street Common, though the 10 bus route along Victoria Park Road was also affected.

In the mid-1970s huge road schemes were proposed that, if implemented, would have bisected central Hackney by a four-lane road from Hackney Wick to Dalston. Opposition was considerable, but then this report appeared in the Hackney Gazette *of 22 April 1975.*

SURVEY SHOCK ON TRAFFIC PLAN – RESIDENTS VOTE 'YES' FOR NEW HIGHWAY
The controversial plans for a four-lane road from Hackney Wick to Dalston have been given a decisive go-ahead by local residents. The surprise results of an independent survey show 70% in favour of the highway – despite vigorous campaigning by pressure groups.

Only five per cent came out against the GLC's six point package to improve traffic in the borough of which the road is an essential part. The apparent truth about how local residents really feel was revealed in a survey carried out for Hackney by a reputable firm of market researchers, who asked the views of well over a thousand people. They have put the council in somewhat of a dilemma as it had pledged to carry out the wishes of the electorate. Strong protests from groups like the Stop the Road Campaign and Hackney Trades Council had suggested that popular opinion was against the road.

However opponents were quick to claim that residents could only agree to the whole package, and were not able to support parts and not others. The findings

A *Hackney Gazette* reporter talking to Susan Attersall (centre) and Carol Blair in Graham Road about the planned four-lane road for central Hackney, 1975.

contrasted with the views of 400 people who had turned up to a local meeting, and where all except one or two were against the road. The Gazette's own investigations showed that local people who lived on the route were not aware of the full implications of the scheme.

Although the new road was not built, traffic continued to be a problem in Dalston, as lorries used it as a through route. One morning in May 1981 sixty protesters gathered at a pedestrian crossing on Graham Road at 7 a.m. and blocked the road for half an hour to demonstrate in favour of road restrictions. On the plus side, 1980 saw the opening of new stations on the North London line at Hackney Wick and Hackney Central, the high-point of a £3 million scheme intended to improve transport routes deemed vital to support the regeneration of London's Docklands.

BEATING THE PARKING PROBLEM?

One way to beat the parking problem, as spotted by the *Hackney Gazette* in April 1970.

Some wide-awake prize-winners at Scawfell School, July 1957.

The majority of school reports tended to be of openings, sanitized visits or the comments of worthies on speech days, although the latter have a certain social resonance. Speaking at Shoreditch College for the garment trade's annual prize-giving in November 1953, the principal, Mrs D.M. Glasswell, focused her attentions downwards, as the Hackney Gazette *of 6 November reported:*

'Appalling' numbers of girls have flat feet, and the wearing of shoes with sling-backs, wedge heels or no heels at all is to blame, declared Mrs Glasswell. . . . She urged parents to ensure that their young daughters wore sensible shoes.

In July 1957 the headmaster of Scawfell Secondary School, Shoreditch, felt that many of his pupils arrived at school only half awake and Shoreditch's LCC member who awarded the school prizes felt that television 'does pull at bit'. In December 1963, though, there was no doubt in the mind of the Mayor of Shoreditch, the Revd Meredith Davies, also Shoreditch's Rector and Rural Dean, as he presented prizes at Shoreditch School in Falkirk Street:

Before presenting the prizes he took a verbal swipe at the tendency of some boys to dress and have haircuts like the Beatles. He exhorted teenagers to be individuals. [He] was anxious to point out that he had no quarrel with the Beatles themselves, but he complained that their haircuts were causing 'the trouble'.

'You can be as good and much better than the Beatles, but don't copy that style', he stressed with a smile. Similar advice was offered to girls, persuading them against being 'with it' at the expense of losing their individuality. . . .

Not all educational reports focused on the negative. In 1950 an exhibition at Queensbridge Secondary School surprised visitors who discovered that both boys and girls were taught cookery and woodwork:

Handicrafts are linked at the school with the teaching of some important subjects such as history and drama. There were some remarkable models tracing the

development of housing and transport from primitive times. Specimens of pottery and puppetry also aroused curiosity and attention. A large scale model of St Alban's Abbey was . . . prominent . . . and much interest was taken by visitors in photographs of the school's most recent camp at Hindhead.

How different from this complaint of the cost of local education, which appeared in a local paper in 1888:

'Dame Sybil Thorndike speaks up' at the opening of Benthal Road Primary School, November 1949.

Tomorrow a reduction of one halfpenny in the school Board rate is to be announced. I am glad to hear it. The estimates will be £40,000 loss with many thousand more children in attendance. I go for economy with efficiency; but how about efficiency, if the following answers given at a recent London School Board examination are to be taken as criteria:

'Where is Turkey?' – Turkey is the capital of Norfolk.

'Where is Gibraltar?' – Gibberalter is the principle town in Rooshia.

'What do you know of the patriarch Abraham?' – he was the father of Lot and had two wives; he kept wun at home and he turned t'other into the desert, where she became a pillow of salt in the daytime and a pillow of fire at nite.

'Give the names of the books of the Old Testament.' – Devonshire, Exeter, Littikus, Numbers, Stronomy, Jupiter, Judges, Ruth etc.

'Who was Moses?' – He was an Egypshion. He lived in a bark maid of bullrushers and he kep a golden carf, and he worshipt braizen snakes, and he het nuthing but kwales and manner for forty years. He was kort by the hair of his head while riding under the bow of a tree, and he was killd by his son Absalon as he was a-hanging from the bow. His end was pease.

Are these results really worth the 8*d* in the pound, besides school fees, that the people of London are called upon to pay?

CHAPTER SIX

LAW AND ORDER

Hackney Mercury, 20 March 1886

Energetic action is being taken by a sub-committee of the Hackney Vestry with the assistance of Mr Richard Ellis, the able legal adviser of that body, to cope with the growing evil arising from the increase in the number of disorderly houses in the neighbourhood of Dalston and if possible to stamp out what is nothing more or less than a social disgrace to the parish in which it exists. A brief review of the work undertaken and the results obtained . . . may be interesting to those of our readers who sympathise with the spread of social purity and the extermination of every kind of vice.

There follows a summary of the report of the special committee on disorderly houses, reporting on four convictions. A list of a further twenty-one names was handed to the police, though the majority of the houses were found to be empty. The report continued:

Attention has also been given to the nuisance caused by street prostitution, but this being a matter over which the local authorities have no control, the clerk was again directed to communicate with the commissioner of Police, but up to the present no official reply has been received further than an interview with the Chief Inspector at Dalston. . . .

Verbatim accounts of correspondence with the Commissioner of Police follow, taken from the reports of local police Inspector Holland and Superintendent Sherlock on the activities of James Grant of 19 Somerford Grove, where two known local prostitutes lived. The letter continued:

Observation has been kept on the house between the hours of 7pm and 2am by Police constable Brown since the 18th inst., as directed, during which time several females, all known prostitutes, have been seen to enter with men nightly and leave together after staying a short time. On the 24th inst. the occupier removed his furniture and left the neighbourhood and the house is now empty.

Local people took matters into their own hands and:

. . . several of the inhabitants of Dalston formed themselves into a Vigilance Committee, of which Mr R.C. Hull of Forest-road, Dalston was appointed the hon sec. This committee interviewed the local authorities and the Vestry appointed a Special Committee to take the matter up. At a meeting of the Special Committee a member of the vigilance Committee handed in a list of houses, at the same time stating that they were known . . . to be occupied by persons who used them for immoral purposes.

Further action by the police followed.

Hackney Gazette, 26 January 1894

HORSE STEALING AT STAMFORD HILL

Yesterday at London County Sessions before Sir Forest Fulton Q.C, Henry Riley, twenty three, dealer, was indicted for having stolen a horse value £8, the property of George Leighton.

Mr Purcell prosecuted.

The prosecutor turned a grey mare out to graze in a field at Stamford hill, and on going to see it on Dec 30, he found that it was gone. He at once gave information to the police, who in the course of their inquiry found that the horse had been taken to a slaughter yard at Stratford and sold for 16s. The prisoner's defence was that he had obtained the horse for a brown one, which he had exchanged with a man whom he did not know.

The jury found him guilty.

Detective-sergeant Edwards proved a previous conviction of five years for horse stealing.

Detective Simmonds said prisoner was a companion of horse thieves and that during the last three months he had taken no less than eleven horses to the Marshgate slaughter yard at Stratford.

Sir Forest Fulton sentenced him to five years penal servitude.

Hackney Gazette, 22 November 1901

HOAX ON LOCAL PUBLICAN AND TRADESMEN

The authorities at Dalston lane police-station have received information from a local publican and a number of leading tradesmen of the district of a wholesale hoax played upon them last week.

It appears that Mr H.R. Wilkinson of the King's Arms, High Street, Kingsland, advertised for a barman, asking applicants to apply between 11 and 1 o'clock. There was a good response to the advertisement, with the result that he was suited before the hour stated. Three applicants put in an appearance, but were thanked and told that the post had been filled up. At this the men seemed to take offence, one of them stating that he had been put to much inconvenience. The result has been the hoaxing, not only of the landlord, but of persons of various trades and professions – butchers, bakers, barbers, friend fish merchants, undertakers and doctors.

An undertaker, who was called upon, was told by the man that he was the manager of the King's Arms and that his wife, aged 32, had just died, and that he wished the undertaker to make the necessary arrangements for the funeral. On going to the house, the undertaker found the supposed corpse alive and well, serving behind the bar, in her customary genial style. When leaving the house, he met another of his trade, about to enter, upon whom the same joke had been played, the order having been given to three undertakers in all.

Shortly after, a local butcher arrived on the scene with some loin chops, followed by two other members of his fraternity, one with a leg of pork and the other with several steaks. Then came a local corset makers' assistant, with half a dozen pairs of corsets, and a draper's assistant with a large parcel of ladies' underclothing.

Kingsland High Street, 1905.

A cheesemonger's assistant then turned up with a quarter of cheese cut up into penny-worths for sale in the bar. A doctor from Stamford hill also drove up post haste to attend to a person who was supposed to be seriously ill, and a tailor came to take the measurements for three suits in black. A bootmaker with several pairs of boots and shoes came to wait upon what he deemed a good customer, whilst a large supply of crockery was also deposited in the house of the astonished landlord.

But the pleasurable excitement was rudely interrupted by the arrival of a member of the hair dressing fraternity, who announced that he had just come to shave the corpse. The weather just now being exceedingly cold, a ton of coals was ordered from a local merchant, whilst a second undertaker arrived to tender his services to the bereaved family. Numerous other orders were stopped by the landlord sending round to warn tradesmen of the doings of these men who sought to be funny at other people's expense.

The articles, which were all paid for on delivery, also included a dish of fried fish, a bath, a pair of steps and some rugs.

The following letter was received by Mr Wilkinson on Friday morning Great Britain [sic] 14,11,1901, Dear Sir, – I replied to your advertisement this morning and found you were suited – before the prescribed time, thereby putting me to a great inconvenience. In return for which I thought I would send you a little present, namely steak, lino, boots, harp, umbrellas, hardware, mourning suits, leg of pork, mutton chops, fried fish, baker, newsagent, greengrocer, cheesemonger, doctor, barber for shaving corpse, two undertakers to bury a —— like you. Hoping you will soon be dead, I remain, yours truly, A Universal provider Out of Work.

Naturally the tradesmen in question are much incensed at such a practical joke, which has caused them a great deal of inconvenience and would like to see the offenders brought to justice.

Durlston Road, looking towards the Geldeston Road junction, *c.* 1920.

Hackney Gazette, April 1901

CLAPTON SHOOTING CASE. EXTRAORDINARY ESCAPE FROM DEATH

Charles Henry Sutcliffe, 22 of 56 Durlston-road, Upper Clapton, was charged on Saturday at the North London Police-court, before Mr Fordham with attempting to commit suicide by shooting himself in the head with a revolver at 28 Durlston-road.

Mr Alfred James Verdon, traveller, of 56 Durlston-road said that the accused was his brother-in-law. He had been residing at the witness' address, but during the absence of another brother-in-law who resided at no 28, he had been sleeping at that house. At 11.30 on Thursday night while walking with his wife in Northwold-road witness met the prisoner. Witness said 'What is up with you? Come, buck up and let's go home.'

They all proceeded to No 28 Durlston road and went to the bedroom, where Mrs Verdon made the bed. They stayed about half an hour and when they left the prisoner came down and let them out. Mrs Verdon stood talking at the door, while witness went on. As his wife did not follow, witness went back. She was standing by the gate and she said 'Jim, a revolver has just gone off.' The front door was at that time shut and bolted. The prisoner, in answer to the witness' loud knocking came down and opened the door. He then seemed quite sober. Witness noticed a black patch on the prisoner's forehead, and he asked him what he had done. He replied 'I am shot. I have shot myself.' On going into the bedroom, witness found a six-chambered revolver on the dressing table. Taking this up he ran out of the house for a doctor and the police. The revolver belonged to the owner of the house and had been left there as a protection against burglars.

Mrs Minnie Verdon said that when she made the bed she found the revolver among the bedclothes, and placed it on the dressing-table at the end of the bed. She said 'Goodbye' to her brother and he locked up the house. When she got to the gate she heard a shot. On the prisoner opening the door again she said 'You did not shoot yourself, did you?' He replied, 'I don't know. It must have gone off.'

Dr H.J. Buck of 23 Clapton Common also gave evidence. On examining Sutcliffe, Buck found a bullet lying on the surface of the frontal bone.

He extracted it and found that the surface had been flattened by striking against the bone. Fortunately the bone in that part of the forehead was very thick. The revolver was no toy. It must have been held close to the head and when fired the bullet could not have attained its full speed or the bone would have been penetrated and the man killed instantly. The prisoner had been drinking and was in a dazed state but not drunk. Probably the shock had subdued him. When the wound had been dressed the constable asked him if he could take him down to the station and witness assented. The prisoner walked down the stairs without assistance. He then asked if he could smoke, and concluding that it would do him no harm witness told him he might. He then rolled a cigarette as coolly and cleverly as Mrs Martin Harvey did in 'The Cigarette Maker.'

Sutcliffe later remembered nothing of the incident and was committed for trial as suicide was a criminal offence at the time. Before he was taken away the magistrate asked the doctor if he had noticed any mental defect in Sutcliffe.

The doctor thought the accused must be a little thick headed in more senses than one. Beyond unexpected complications which might arise in connection with the wound, the prisoner was none the worse for it. It was a most fortunate escape from death.

August–September 1911 – Hackney Downs
The following edited pieces are from the Stoke Newington Recorder *and supplemented with diary entries from the scrapbook of Presbyterian minister William Cross.*
    To the Editor of the Recorder, *August 1911.*

Dear Sir,
I venture to ask your kind help in an effort to grapple with a public evil.

There is a plague spot. It is called Hackney Downs. The spectacle to be seen on Hackney Downs is no secret. On the wide spaces of the grass at night scores, if not hundreds, of couples resort, lying about shamelessly in attitudes suggesting nothing save unworthy and corrupting conduct. This is flagrant and increasing.

Along the pathways and on the borders of this vicious spectacle, large crowds of young men and women squander their time in frivolity. Is it surprising that these are constantly tempted to throw off all restraint, and that cases of destroyed moral life are frequent?

No one seems to protest. No one warns. The churches meekly open their doors. Respectable people pass. Night comes down. The restraints of light is withdrawn. Then from dusk to midnight all restraint, all modesty, all reverence is gone! The decencies of life are openly flouted.

Who benefits? Those whose evil trade it is to sell body and soul for vicious indulgence. The slackness of public interference is made a cloak and shelter for their vile traffic. Who suffers? The whole populace. Some, as soon as they can, leave the neighbourhood rather than run the risk of bringing their children near such a CESSPOOL.

Hackney Downs, 1905.

We have a right to ask that the place be better lighted, and that it shall be made illegal for people to lie about on the grass after dusk, and that the footpaths shall be strictly supervised by the police. If we cannot cleanse the Augean stable of vice, for people will do wrong if they are determined, we can at least insist that it be removed from our neighbourhood.

Yours sincerely,

William Cross

Minister of Clapton Presbyterian Chapel

Editorial from the Stoke Newington Recorder, *August 1911.*

Whilst regretting the necessity for so doing, we willingly publish the letter from the rev. William Cross; in his zeal to remedy an undoubted evil, our correspondent has been guilty of an extravagance of language. To describe one of our most popular open space as 'a cesspool' is, to say the least, an exaggeration and will be regarded by many as a slur on the women of Hackney.

By removing couples from Hackney Downs, the evil will not be eliminated, but simply transferred elsewhere. The only real effectual cure is the cultivation of character in the home and a little practical Christianity on the part of ministers of all denominations.

Letter to the Revd Cross, 1 September 1911 from 4 Sach Road, Upper Clapton.

Well done Mr Cross!!

All right thinking people must be at your back and support you in this courageous attack you have made on this disgraceful state of affairs.

If the late Rector of Hackney were still here, he would be willing to take the lead in a public meeting of protest. The thing must be grappled with now.

With very kind and warm regards

A.B. French

Dear Sir,

As the Mayor, I do not as a rule enter into the discussion of controversial subjects in the Press, but the letter of the Rev. William Cross calls for a reply in the interests of the borough.

Mr Cross in common with others has sometimes seen evil where none existed and that in many instances what he has observed is merely an expression of affection between persons who may be guilty of lack of refinement jarring to sensitive minds, but who are not guilty of the gross misconduct attributed to them.

There is of course occasionally grounds for complaint. Places of public resort like the Downs must sometimes be abused by persons whose conduct is offensive to the great majority who make a legitimate use of them, and the Borough Council is in sympathy with any attempt to suppress misconduct by persons of this class.

It must be recollected that Hackney Downs is an open space dedicated to the use of the public, and that there is no power to prevent persons from lying on the grass if they desire to do so. To make this illegal, as your correspondent suggests, would deprive many tired persons of a well-earned rest, and place needless restriction on the majority of well behaved citizens.

I am, dear sir,

W.F. Fenton-Jones

Mayor

Extract from the diary of William Cross.

On Tuesday 5th September 1911, I called upon Superintendent Mackay at Clapton Police Station. He is a big, powerful, splendid fellow. He received me kindly. I told him the Mayor has asked me to call upon him and I assured him I thoroughly appreciated the difficulty of the work the police had to do on the Downs; and that I believed they did their work well. He told me that in his judgement, Hackney Downs was one of the cleanest places in London. 'Why' he said 'go to Hyde park, Hampstead Heath, Hackney Marshes; they are perfect brothels compared to Hackney Downs.' It was a shock to me, a horrible, ghastly shock. London is a sodom. I came away, saddened and sickened at the thought of the city where I live.

To the Editor of the Recorder, *September 1911.*

Sir,

I did my courting on the Downs for five years and I can assure you I never saw any indecency or immodesty. We still go over there late in the evening to take the dog for a run. She delights in scampering over these 'sprawling couples' whom I often find are fast asleep. They are rather close, but only those with dirty minds would attribute any evil to them. Young girls work very long hours in stuffy workrooms and young men, being mostly on their feet all day long, are dead tired; and there are not enough seats on the Downs to accommodate these 'hundreds' of couples – so they resort to the grass.

People at the seaside 'sprawl' about both day and night, but no-one sees anything 'suggestive' in that. There are men creeping about trying to find the evil that exists solely in their own minds.

May I beg of these prigs to let the couples spoon while they can; their troubles will start all too soon; and who has any right to say they attend no church or chapel? I suggest that Mr Cross should go and speak to these 'indecent sprawling couples' and present them with a nice little tract. To call an affectionate attitude 'compromising' is wicked and disgusting.

If the spaces are closed, put plenty of seats for couples, both young and old, to sit or rest or spoon. They only have the evenings.

Yours faithfully,

One of the Couples on the grass.

An editorial from the Stoke Newington Recorder *for 15 September 1911 may serve to close this selection from a very extensive correspondence. The editorial supported local people being able to sit on the grass. After all,*

Young people will be young people and larkish and will indulge in vulgarities. Some sit on gates and stiles, others on the couch in the front room, others spoon in the doorway at night with the old man calling down the stairs wanting to know 'are you going to keep Bessie at the door all night?' Most people have been through the moon struck stage at some point in their lives and there is no shame indecency or immodesty in it.

The piece concludes with the verse from the Rubyiat of Omar Khyam where the poet is seated with a loaf of bread beneath the tree (presumably on the grass), with a flask of wine and a loved one:

The old rascal – what was in his mind and in the wilderness too? It is a good job he didn't live round the Downs or else goodness what the passers by might think!

Hackney Gazette, 2 January 1914
VANISHED CLAPTON SHARE-OUT. 'THE DIDDLUM CLUB' SECRETARY AND MISSING MONEY
At the North London Police Court, John Thomas Scrase, 36, described as a window cleaner of Pedro-street, Clapton Park, was charged before Mr Chester Jones with fraudulently converting various sums of money paid into a loan club of which he was the secretary and treasurer to his own use.

Two witnesses, George Smith and Mrs Sarah Andrews, testified paying in money. Smith paid in £2 13s 1½d and had expected to receive his pay out on 29 December but Scrase did not show up. Scrase claimed that he could only remember one or two of the last few days. His mind was a blank.

Detective-sergeant Young stated that the prisoner was secretary and treasurer of the 'Diddlum Club'.

Mr Chester Jones: 'I think "diddlum" means to do you out of something.' (Laughter)

The officer said that the amount paid in by the members was £51 odd. On the 20th the prisoner's wife reported that he was 'missing'.

Scrase gave himself up at Dalston police station where he claimed:

'My head is a blank. I had a bag with ever so much money in it. I met a man and woman who took me into an empty house and I lost the money. I don't know who they were.'

One of the witnesses, Arthur Niblett, was recalled to the stand:

. . . and was asked by the prisoner: 'When you paid me had you any idea I was going to run away with the money?' Witness: 'No.'

Mr Chester Jones: 'He would not have paid you if he had.' (Laughter)

Scrase was remanded for doctor's report, and on reading it Jones concluded he was faced by a case of shamming and remanded Scrase for a week for him to find the lost club money.

Hackney Gazette, 9 January 1970

SEARCH FOR PUB GUNMAN. CASE OF MISTAKEN IDENTITY, SAYS SHOOTING VICTIM

Last night Hackney detectives, led by Detective Inspector John Groves, were appealing to Gazette readers for help in tracing a blue Dormobile-type van used in Tuesday night's shooting at the Royal Standard public house, Victoria Park Road, South Hackney.

Victim Brian Boswell had thirty two pellets in his leg and described what happened from his bed in Bethnal Green hospital.

The shooting occurred . . . soon after opening time. Mrs Boswell's mother was doing her usual Tuesday night stint behind the bar when the gunman walked in. She saw her son gunned down together with [Alan] Bennett. Brian shouted to his mother 'Get down behind the bar'. The bar was empty except for a third customer who escaped injury.

'The gunshot blew the stool from under me' Brian Boswell told a Gazette reporter. 'I fell to the floor and crawled through to the other bar. I heard the man fire another shot which hit the ceiling. Then we waited on the floor until the bar was clear'. Added Mr Boswell 'I never even knew that he had hit me, I just had a tingling feeling in my leg. It must be a case of mistaken identity. I have never seen the man in my life before.' The only description he could give of the man was that he was short with a hat pulled down over his face.

Boswell had been a regular in the Royal Standard for ten years and said that there had never been any trouble there before not even a fight. Landlord Joseph Smith was upstairs watching the 'Today' programme at the time.

He added 'Little did I think at the time that the next day the "Today" crew would be in my bar and featuring the pub on its programme!'

Hackney Gazette, 22 August 1975

TEST SABOTEUR SUSPECT STRIPS OFF – NUDE TARZAN ACT BY FRIEND OF GEORGE DAVIS

Colin Dean, self confessed saboteur of the third cricket Test match at Headingley, was arrested in Victoria Park yesterday morning after streaking naked and leaping through the trees like Tarzan.

The 37 year old unemployed labourer surprised early morning strollers when he stripped off his clothes and waded nude into the park's ornamental lake.

Police watched as Dean, one of the leading campaigners to get his brother-in-law George Davis released from a 20 year prison sentence, stood waist deep in water.

Eventually two officers started rowing to the island. Dean saw them coming and fled to the shore where he clambered up another tree and from a high branch did Tarzan impressions and dared police to try and grab him.

Davis had been sentenced for armed robbery and injuring a policeman at a time when he claimed to have been driving his mini-cab. 'George Davis is innocent okay' slogans appeared all over the Hackney area in the mid-1970s. Dean, who had damaged the pitch at Headingly by digging it up, was finally captured by police and taken to Bow Street station for questioning.

Vicar Donald Pateman.

Hackney Gazette, 6 March 1981

The late Donald Pateman, vicar of St Mark's Church, Dalston, was well known for his forthright opinions, though not all his views made the front page. However, his bid to bring back medieval punishment did.

PUT NASTY LITTLE MUGGERS IN THE STOCK, SAYS VICAR

Only way to make the streets safe, he says.

Muggers and hooligans should be put in the stocks as a punishment for their 'foul' crimes, says a local vicar.

The Rev Donald Pateman called on the forces of law and order to bring back this ancient form of punishment as 'a sure safe painless way of dealing with muggers, hooligans and other lusty young trouble makers'. He declared 'mugging has reached wholly unacceptable proportions.'

And he adds 'It is high time the stocks were reintroduced as a punishment for these nasty little crooks.'

Pateman's views, set forth in his parish magazine, followed attacks two elderly female members of his congregation and were in response to the fear of older people to go out at night. He then listed the advantages of his proposal:

• It would be immediate – a youngster caught mugging on a Monday night would appear at Highbury the next day and with a bit of luck would find himself or herself cooling his or her heels in the stocks by midday Tuesday.

• It would be inexpensive – the borough council has plans to erect a reception centre for 26 nasty little female troublemakers at a cost of £250,000. That's all the centre will hold. My cure would cost £5 for the whole boiling.

• It would be effective – I cannot imagine many youngsters coming back for a second dose once they have suffered a day's boredom in the stocks exposed to the contempt of passers-by.

And he concludes 'Well, worth a try, what?'

Local police refused to comment to the Gazette *on Pateman's proposals.*

Hackney Gazette, 23 March 1982
UPROAR OVER STRIP SHOW AND SEX ACT AT TOWN HALL CLUB

An angry demonstration failed to bring the curtains down on a strip show at Hackney Town Hall's social club.

Police cut a swathe through 70 demonstrators to allow members and guests of the council's social club into the show unhindered.

The town hall's white collar union NALGO and other pressure groups picketed the performance in a bid to turn the audience away.

They objected to the entertainment, arguing that striptease degrades women and encourages men to treat them as sex objects.

And they argued that Hackney Council – which has a public commitment to equality between men and women – should not allow it to go ahead on its premises.

Love Scene

The strip act was part of a stag night show featuring comedians and music for male members of the Hackney Borough Social Club held at the Town Hall last Friday.

Further controversy blew up after reports that the strippers' act culminated in simulated scenes of lesbian love making.

When asked if the reports were true, a member of the audience replied 'They are not entirely untrue.'

Spokesman for the NALGO pickets, John Rehan, said the union found striptease in itself objectionable and would not object any more if the reports were true.

But the social club secretary Brian Blackler said there would be an urgent inquiry into the claims.

Mr Blackler, who did not attend the show, commented 'I would be absolutely astonished if these claims were true. It would have been quite the contrary to what was intended. I will be making inquiries as a matter of urgency.'

He said that the social club committee, which contains five councillors and representatives from the town hall trade unions, would reconsider its policy on strip shows in the light of the protests.

Idiots

Councillor Reg Crowfoot, who attended the stag night, dismissed the demonstrators as a 'load of idiots.' He suggested that their energy would be better devoted to their work than to protests about strip shows.

When asked about the conclusion of the strippers' act, he said he could not comment as he was in the bar at the time.

CHAPTER SEVEN

WAR

The colonial wars of the nineteenth century did not have a great impact on Hackney, but the Boer War was a different matter. Among those British forces serving in South Africa were the Hackney Volunteers and this report of their home-coming forms a useful summary of their experience of war.

THE RETURN OF THE HACKNEY VOLUNTEERS. AN ENTHUSIASTIC RECEPTION. STIRRING SCENES, JUNE 1901

After a period of somewhat anxious waiting on the part of their relatives and friends, the Hackney Volunteers who offered their services to the War Office at a critical time in our country's history, arrived home safely on Wednesday evening and were most enthusiastically welcomed. The reception was well-deserved, for although none of the twenty-eight men who left at duty's call lost their lives in actual warfare, the Volunteers took part in several trying engagements, and were present at the

A carnival float in Stoke Newington Church Street, possibly at the end of the Boer War, 1901.

battles of Honing Spirit and Rhenosterkop. They also formed part of the force who occupied Pretoria and were complimented by Lord Roberts upon their smartness and bravery. The men left Hackney for Warley in the early part of February 1900, and from thence soon departed for South Africa, where they landed in the latter part of March. . . . It is a matter for congratulation that only two of their number died during the campaign, Col-Sergt. Miller succumbing to enteric fever at Bloemfontein and Private J. Rogers dying of the same disease. The latter's brother, T.W. Rogers, went through the same trying campaign safely. It is expected that each one of the returned Volunteers will be presented with a medal and five bars. . . .

The Volunteers were met at Hackney Downs station by a large crowd, who included Viscount Horncastle, the Mayor of Hackney, and they then marched to the Town Hall via the densely crowded Amhurst Road and Mare Street. Inside the Town Hall were Volunteers of the 4th Essex Regiment and a brass band. After speeches the band played Home Sweet Home and Auld Lang Syne, finishing with God Save the King. After a short march to the Drill Hall, the soldiers dispersed.

The First World War had greater effect on the district. In its first issue after the outbreak of war, on 7 August 1914, the Hackney & Stoke Newington Recorder *reported the patriotic announcements of the mayors of Hackney and Stoke Newington, which included statements of support for the new £1 and 10s notes, notice of a service of intercession at St Mary's Church, Stoke Newington, and guards from the National Reserve round the electricity generating station at Stoke Newington. Hackney's works were protected by the Council's own workforce. There were also reports of panic food buying and rumours of the imminent closure of the German Hospital, although it actually remained open. However, more disturbing were local reactions to the large resident German community, which had been established in Hackney since the mid-nineteenth century.*

ANTI GERMAN RIOTS. LAST NIGHT IN CLAPTON
A more sinister side of the general temperament of the local population was last night manifested in Clapton with serious effects. A demonstration which took place in Chatsworth-road, and was actively participated in by a crowd of well over five thousand people comprehended at one time a situation of extreme gravity. . . . [I]t would appear that a German baker, Henry Lunken, who during the course of many years' residence in North London, has become a naturalized Englishman, has found his business greatly to prosper. His substantial profits have been devoted over that period to the purchase of property in the neighbourhood . . . and it is stated to be the fact that concurrently with the recent rise in the bank rate, Mr Lunken had decided upon substantial increase in the rent to the tenants of his property. He is said to have given as the reason for the latter the existence of war between Germany and England. At any rate, whether from this or other reasons, Mr Lunken was the object of an anti German demonstration last night which assumed such serious proportions that a heavy force of police of the J division with truncheons drawn were drafted from head quarters to the spot. . . .

The Lunken family outside their shop at 71 Chatsworth Road, 1913.

WRECKING A HANDSOME SHOP

Mr Lunken is the proprietor of the shop, No 71 Chatsworth-road, . . . one of the best fitted out in the neighbourhood. It possesses a handsome frontage and the interior is replete with plate glass mirrors, electric lights and every modern accessory of an enterprising and successful business. At dusk last night a large number of persons, said to be the tenants, found their way into the thoroughfare. The mischief of their intent was pretty quickly evidenced by the smashing of Mr Lunken's shop windows. . . . The fast increasing crowd proceeded to wreak their ill-will by heaving brick-bats at the upper windows of the premises occupied . . . by the German and his family. The crowd and the uproar rapidly grew . . . and a body of uniformed men were . . . despatched [from Clapton police station].

By the time of their arrival the riot had assumed most serious dimensions. Chatsworth-road was crowded from end to end with an immense mob of people, flourishing miniature Union Jacks and shouting various patriotic songs, with which were alternated booings for the unfortunate German and flinging showers of missiles at his premises by the angry crowds, necessitating the reinforcement of the police, who eventually formed cordons across the road at various points, thus intersecting the crowd and eventually leading to the quietening down of an anti German riot which threatened at one time most serious consequences.

On Wednesday a somewhat similar demonstration was made against a German in Kingsland-road, who, during the afternoon was seen, flying in terror from one of the adjacent courts into the main street. He was pursued by a crowd of angry women, who abused and pelted him unmercifully. With his clothing torn almost to tatters and his face streaming with blood, the unfortunate man made a dash to gain a stationary tramcar and despite the frenzied efforts of the women to pull him off, he managed to gain the top deck of the car. He was, however, followed by several of the infuriated women, who continued the attack on him as the car moved on, to such an extent that the conductor advised the man to leave the car at Shoreditch, and this he found himself able to do, darting, an utter wreck, down a by-street and escaping from his enemies.

There were more anti-German riots later in the war. In May 1915, the news of the sinking of the Lusitania *by a German submarine resulted in a night of rioting and damage to over seventy German shops, which were looted. What started again in the Chatsworth Road area spread west to Wilton Road and Kingsland Road and the mob marched down Balls Pond Road towards Islington to the Angel.*

Letters from soldiers were published. Rifleman E.J. Swift was a Stoke Newington Territorial and this is an extract from his account of the first battle of Ypres, in October/November 1914.

We were taken to a field which we reached in grey dawn and were given food and a few hours rest, with orders to hold ourselves in readiness to advance at any moment. We, of course, had no definite news, but conjectured a lot, especially as stragglers from the front continually passed us, and blood stained weary men and stretcher-bearers made a procession of agony before our eyes. At last we advanced to support a battalion of regulars moving forward. A hurricane of shells swished in and over us, and took their dreadful toll. The constant shock of explosions made the earth round quake and the air was agitated and filled with noxious fumes. It was awful. The din pierced one's ears and almost deafened. The Germans were evidently making a supreme effort to break through and their concentrated artillery was

The Stoke Newington Volunteer Corps band, 1917.

The Stoke Newington Volunteer Corps in training at Tadsworth, near Epsom, 1917.

crumbling away the khaki wall opposing them. . . . I saw parties of our men who staggered about as if drunk, stupefied and weakened and in many cases dying in batches [in the aftermath of gas attacks]. For the first time during the war I believe, it was a fight in the open. The Germans came over the sky-line in front of us like a swarm of ants. Our artillery and our machine guns belched death and . . . they turned tail and scampered back. We were scarce of men . . . so we entrenched ourselves and awaited the German attack.

An artillery bombardment followed during which an officer friend of Swift was slightly injured.

It had been raining heavily the previous night and we were standing feet deep in mud and our drenched clothes were steaming in the morning sun. The bombardment never ceased and continued while we were relieved by fresh troops.

As they retired Swift noted countless carcasses of horses along the road, and the destroyed and burning houses.

It was a lurid picture, conflagration all around, flaring and flickering throughout the night, and emitting stenches of smouldering straw. Dark figures of moving men silhouetted against the blaze – troops, guns and human derelicts painfully travelling in the direction of dressing stations. And above all the nerve fraying shrieks of shells and their shuddering explosions. The remnants of our battalion expected to be hit. We had been relieved from the firing line, only to be battered about in our place of imagined security. A lot of our fellows were lost in that 'resting' field. A little group of us were cleaning rifles behind a mound of earth, and having become accustomed to the noise of shells, we had . . . grown fatalistic. Suddenly a terrific blinding explosion lifted us and flung us about like skittles. Six out of eight of us were hit, some of the poor chaps receiving as many as five wounds. I got a crashing blow on the head from a fragment of shell and my wound, though not dangerous, bled profusely. We were then taken across to the dressing station and bandaged and then sent farther down the road to a place of concentration for the wounded.

From there, still in danger from shells, Swift and the other wounded were taken by Red Cross convoy to a Canadian hospital and after further dressing and a meal taken outside the battlefield. On the way they passed back through Ypres.

Only a fortnight previously we had marched through its streets, admiring its fine buildings. Now it is a crumbled mass of ruins, simply piles of bricks and twisted girders . . . and . . . deserted except for motor ambulances darting and dodging around shell holes, dead horses and pieces of masonry littering the roadway.

Swift ended up in Boulogne prior to dispatch back to England.

Military action was not confined to the battlefields in Europe. On 31 May 1915 the Germans launched the first air raid on London, when Zeppelin Airship LZ38, piloted by Major D. Erich Linnarz, took off on a course that took it over Hackney and Stoke Newington. Linnarz claimed that the intended target was the waterworks. In a retrospective piece of 15 July 1938, the North London Recorder *takes up the story:*

It was just after eleven o'clock on May 31 that Major Linnarz . . . released the mechanism which held his weapons of death.

Mr Blackmore, present assistant librarian of Stoke Newington, remembers it very well. He heard the Zeppelin come overhead, heard the mighty crash of the bomb as it fell in Alkham-road. He rushed out to see what had happened. But there was not much to see. The bomb had gone clean through the roof.

A sleeping child in the house survived unscathed, although the top floor of the house was destroyed. Blackmore's account continued:

'The Dynevor-road area was more spectacular. Here Linnarz had done a better job of work. The streets at the back of the present Recorder offices were sprayed by bombs.

One fell in Neville-road, several in Mildmay-road, another at No 33 Cowper-road. The Cowper-road house was completely gutted by the fire. A little girl lost her life in it and was burnt to death, while her father and four other children were injured. Then the Zeppelin went on to the souther part of the Borough. At St Matthias vicarage, a bomb fell in the front garden, near the gateway.'

After Alkham Road, one bomb fell outside the gas works near Stoke Newington Common (identified as such in the original report, but possibly the author was referring to a gas mantle factory on the High Street, north of Union Street), but failed to explode. Local resident Mrs Clara Gandy of Garnham Road remembered a policeman coming to pick it up and walk away with it. Another 169lb bomb that dropped at the back of the Neville Arms also failed to explode and survived to be photographed with PC Mickey Forbes. It was later officially claimed to be the first enemy bomb dropped on London, although this dubious honour actually belonged to the Alkham Road bomb.

Later air raids were undertaken by Gotha bombers, including the daylight strike on 7 July 1917. One was shot down but between twenty and thirty got through. The City of London was

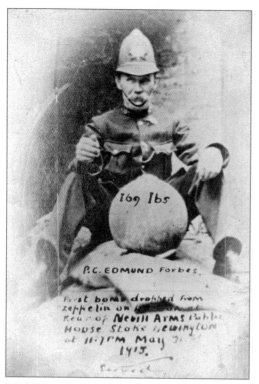

PC Mickey Forbes of Brodia Road, sitting with the unexploded bomb that dropped at the back of the Neville Arms, May 1915. It was claimed as the first enemy bomb dropped on London.

attacked, but houses in Pedro Street, Southwold Road and Reighton Road, Cowper Road and shops facing Palatine Road were all hit, while the Vicar of St Matthias had another bomb fall in his garden. But it was Boleyn Road that bore the worst of the raid. The Hackney & Stoke Newington Recorder *of 23 and 30 May recorded these events.*

The dwellers in that block of houses opposite Ridge's Food factory were all hard working people of the industrial class and the wife of a carman tells how she stood behind the door leading from her front bed sitting room to the kitchen, holding her baby in her arms and her three other children holding on to her skirt. In that way they escaped injury, although the woman was hurt in the face and hands and the windows were blown out, the pictures shaken from the walls and the door splintered by fragments of the bomb.

An adjoining house was wrecked, one woman killed and a mother and her twins buried under rubble. But a large bomb also hit Ridge's Food Mills. A van driver takes up the story:

'We had all been looking through the windows at the approaching aeroplanes and talking of the wonderful sight. When we heard the guns fired and a bomb explode, we decided to go to the back of the premises for safety. We went into the van yard and there found a man and his boy, who had drawn in for safety. There was a gas company's man with his barrow, and he also came into the entrance. We had hardly got there when there was a terrible explosion in the middle of the road. I looked round and there were no casualties among our party

A poster issued by Stoke Newington Borough Council advertising insurance against damage caused by air raids, 1917.

at the back. Luckily there had been some boxes and things between us and the explosion. . . . But the poor vanman and the boy were apparently killed. When we got the horse up he was too badly injured to stand, and fell on the carman again . . . and must have crushed out of the poor fellow all the life there was left in him. The gas company's man had felt the full force of the explosion and was the worst injured of all, so far as I could see. A youth who was passing on a bicycle was absolutely destroyed, portions of his body being blown into our buildings as far as the back wall. . . .'

Frantzman's bakery shop at 154 Boleyn Road was devastated. A girl with a barrow outside had a lucky escape, for although the barrow was destroyed she was merely blown off her feet. However, it was otherwise for Frantzman, another naturalized German living in the area:

. . . for this tradesman, who had a splendid reputation (which never suffered much despite the war) for his generosity to the poor, was killed outright. The ex-German was in the back of his premises, when hearing the sound of the first bomb, near by, he rushed into the shop to protect his daughter, who was serving there. At that moment a second bomb fell, shattering the shop and Frantzman was instantly killed, his daughter injured.

Frantzman's son and housekeeper were also hurt and his journeyman baker, another German, Henry John Hoppe, was killed. In the aftermath of the raid Boleyn Road was a shambles of dead people and horses, smashed carts and a burst water main.

People queuing for potatoes in Shoreditch, 1916. In the face of a potato shortage in the winter of 1916/17, the Mayor of Shoreditch bought 3 tons for the poor of the borough. Police were on hand to keep order.

The Munich Crisis of 1938 accelerated central and local government preparations for civil defence. On 30 September 1938 the Hackney Gazette *reported that the distribution of 90,000 gas masks to Shoreditch Council tenants – private tenants and other householders having to collect theirs from local polling stations – had started. Shelter construction had also begun, although Shoreditch's ARP Officer, Captain Hollis, advised* Gazette *readers that the safest place for people in the event of a raid was indoors. Civil defence also extended to businesses. The* Hackney & Stoke Newington Recorder *of 3 June 1938 reported:*

NEW FACTORY IS BOMB PROOF

Within a few minutes of an air raid, W.J. Bush's new factory in Ash Grove, Hackney, could be cleared of all its machinery and converted into a first aid station.

All machinery on the ground floor is mounted on wheels, could be run right out of the factory within a few minutes of the alarm being given.

The building is heavily built, and its walls and floors are incendiary-bomb proof. It is fitted with air-conditioning plant and is serviced by alternative electricity and water-mains. At one side of the building is a ramp down which stretchers can be run; on the other side is an unloading stage for stretcher cases.

. . . Friday night saw Bush's ARP squads give a demonstration. Smoke bombs were lit in a shed. The firm's fire brigade, the decontamination squad and the first aid party dealt with the 'bombing'.

The confident advice of Captain Hollis was not shared by many Hackney residents, who supported Professor J.B.S. Haldane in his campaign for deep-level bomb shelters for everyone. Haldane spoke at a meeting at the end of January 1939 at Hackney Town Hall, which was organized by the Hackney Trades Council and Borough Labour Party to help publicize a local petition in favour of bomb shelters. Haldane had changed his mind as a result of what he had witnessed in the Spanish Civil War.

The Munich crisis also stimulated a flurry of local activity as wardens went from house to house to supply and fit gas masks, while first-aid posts and decontamination and rescue squads were established and workmen kept busy digging trenches in the parks and open spaces, including on Hackney Downs and the Marshes. Later there was some questioning of the value and purpose of the trenches. Plans were also made for the evacuation of local schools. When war did break out in September 1939, local school children were evacuated from London en masse. On 16 October 1939 the Hackney Gazette *carried a report on a school in Hoxton.*

EVACUATED HOXTON CHILDREN

The lines of Napier-street School, Hoxton, have indeed fallen into pleasant places, for Beechwood School, Leagrave, Luton, where the children are guests for the 'duration', is one of the show schools of the country, and the welcome that staff and scholars received upon their arrival was as kindly as the school was beautiful.

But the Napier School staff and escorts realised soon after their arrival that provision would have to be made for 'running repairs' which the foster mothers could not in fairness be expected to do. They knew too that some of the children had come inadequately clothed, so at once it was decided to do something about it. A flat was taken quite near the school, the landlord made an offer of a weekly contribution in the shape of an allowance on the rent and the staff and escorts not only agreed to make a weekly contribution to cover expenses, but supplied a table, chairs, carpet, a sewing machine and pictures for the walls, and then set to work to make it habitable and efficient for the function it was to perform.

The centre opened on 25 September and in the first fortnight made 191 garments for 77 children, from clothes donated by local people, which were then mended and washed before being handed out.

The varied billeting experiences of evacuated children were not reported. Indeed local worthies were urged to support the cause. Hackney councillor A.E. Hills visited evacuated children from Randall Cremer and Laburnum Street schools in his capacity as chairman of school managers. The Randall Cremer children had gone to Northampton. The Hackney Gazette *of 3 November 1939 covered the story:*

'I found them in a happy and contended condition. I asked them if they wanted to come home and I was told with a great shout "No". The teacher said they were quite pleased with the way the children are behaving and keeping up the name of the school.'

It was more difficult for the teachers of Laburnum Street School, as the children were spread over four villages around Long Buckby. Hills used the Gazette *piece to plead with their mothers to send warm clothing and stout boots and to other readers to donate clothing. Obviously not all mothers had been happy with the evacuation and some had already brought their children back to London. Hill appealed to them:*

'You, by your actions, have robbed your children of their education and the chance of a holiday in the country, where they had an opportunity of learning and improving their knowledge'.

The outbreak of the war curtailed local entertainments. The Stoke Newington Observer *for 12 April 1940 carried a report of a local initiative to meet the challenge:*

Local People get together to provide – MUSIC IN THE BLACKOUT. Famous musicians support big new plan.

When the war came and the streets were blacked out night after night, musical and dramatic activities stopped by the hundred all over London.

In February, concerned at the lack of opportunities for people, particularly young people, to enjoy music and plays and make use of the spare-time the black-out had given them, a Stoke Newington musician, Miss Betty Gordon, of 102 Holmleigh-road, got together with a few friends and a committee was formed.

They aimed at setting up groups where people could sing and play and act and they decided to inaugurate their scheme by an ambitious programme for a two day festival at Stoke Newington Town Hall.

Dame Sybil Thorndike and Alan Bush agreed to be patrons, and Jacob Epstein the artist and playwright Sean O'Casey also supported the festival, which was held on 28 and 29 May. It was intended that the event would lead to the formation of musical groups throughout the district and any profits would go to the Musicians' Benefit Fund.

The Mayor of Hackney does his bit for the drive to collect metal, July 1940.

The early days of the war on the home front also saw the advent of local salvage campaigns. As well as the national drive that saw the loss of much of the borough's iron railings, people were encouraged to hand over scrap metal. On 24 April 1940 the Hackney Gazette *reported on the impact of Hackney's Salvage Exhibition:*

HACKNEY SALVAGE EXHIBITION

A clergyman pushing an ancient lawn mower with a heavy rusty old steel frame and other craps of iron piled on top of it attracted considerable attention as he clattered through Mare-street on Monday. He was making his contribution to the Salvage Exhibition which is being held by Hackney Borough Council this week in an empty shop that originally formed part of Matthew Rose's emporium in the narrow part of Mare-street.

A poor man who makes a living by repairing furniture walked all the way from Leyton to hand in two tins of brass studs from old chairs that he had collected and some boys brought in tin cans.

Hackney people were also encouraged by a mobile daylight cinema van which toured the borough to support the formation of local salvage groups. By August 1940 over 600 tons of metal had been recovered, which besides iron bedsteads, also included German helmets, rifles and other souvenirs of the previous war.

Censorship restricted in-depth reporting on bombing raids during the Second World War, but local papers did carry limited accounts without details of locations. One of the worst incidents of the war was the bomb that fell on Coronation Avenue on the night of

13/14 October 1940, when all five floors of one block of flats were destroyed. Many of the inhabitants were in the shelter in the basement, but all exits were blocked by rubble and it was then flooded by a burst water main. The account of enemy action in the Hackney Gazette for 16 October 1940 described other incidents, including a bomb that fell on a bakery, which had its supply of dough turned into a sticky mess by the effects of an oil bomb. This was how the Coronation Gardens incident was reported:

A considerable number of casualties occurred when a block of flats was hit by an aerial torpedo. The occupants of the flats were under the building when the bomb fell on the pavement, blocking the entrance with masonry and debris. The shelter itself remained intact. Powerful cranes and a fleet of lorries were used to transport the debris away and more than 100 police, troops and wardens were engaged in rescue operations for many hours. The majority of the dead are women and children.

As the rescued people were brought to the road level, they gave the wardens their names and addresses and all the information they could about those remaining below. There were some pitiful scenes. Generally however, the community is bravely facing the catastrophe.

LUCKY ESCAPES
A newsagent said 'I am the luckiest man alive. My father, who is 86, and my mother had used the shelter every night since the bombardment began, but last week I was fortunate to find them a place in the country and had just returned from the station after seeing them off. I had called on a friend and was on the way to the shelter when the explosion occurred. We were blown off our feet, but fortunately escaped injury.'

A woman stated 'While I was in the shelter I remembered I had not fed my cat. So I left the shelter to go to my house which is only a few doors away, when the explosion occurred.'

Others were not so lucky. One woman lost her mother, grandmother, two children and a brother, who were among the 171 people killed.

The new demands on women for essential war work posed a problem for those with children. This report is from the Hackney Gazette of 20 April 1942.

WARTIME DAY NURSERY OPENED. BOON TO HACKNEY WORKING MOTHERS
Hackney's first wartime day nursery for the children of mothers engaged on essential work has been opened at the French Hospital, pleasantly situated on what remains of its once spacious grounds at Victoria Park-road.

A considerable part of the land is now occupied by L.C.C. flats, but the well-kept lawns and garden are retained and on fine days the toddlers and older children will play on the soft turf formerly trodden by the poor and aged descendants of the Huguenot refugees from the beginning of the 18th century [actually only from 1865].

. . . There is accommodation for 50 children under five . . . and it comprises a baby's room, a toddlers' bathroom, a dining and reception room and lavatory on the ground floor; the matron's room, a staff kitchen on the first floor; and a milk room, kitchen, laundry, perambulator store and air raid shelter in the basement.

. . . Each child on arriving at the nursery would be given a bath and changed into nursery clothing and during the day would have three meals cooked on the premises. In the evening the children would be washed and changed into their own clothing ready for their mothers to take them home. The nursery would be open from 7am to 7pm and it was estimated that the cost of each child would be 4s 10d per day, of which the mother would pay 1s per day.

Council staff supplied toys, including a rocking horse supplied by the Municipal Officers Guild. Former mayoress Cllr Mrs C. Gooch hoped that the nursery would survive the war, enabling mothers to have a little recreation or pleasure.

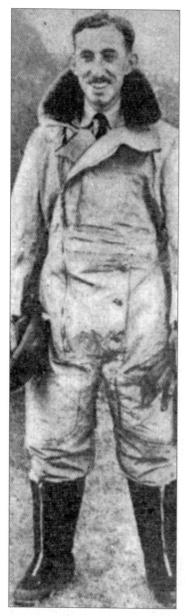

Sergeant Pilot Sydney Cohen, 1943.

During the Second World War the military experiences of those at the front did not feature in the local press as much as they had done during the First World War. Two local men, Walter Roberts of 13 London Fields West Side and Joseph Webb of 23 Belmont Mansions, Goldsmiths Row, were both merchant seamen taken prisoner after the sinking of their merchant ships. On 21 February 1940 the Hackney Gazette *reported their rescue from the German prison ship* Altmark *in Joessing Fjord. Roberts had been taken from the* Doric Star *after it was torpedoed by the German battleship the* Graf Spee *on 2 December 1939. Later in the war one Stoke Newington man gained fame, which was reported in the* Hackney Gazette *on 16 June 1943.*

ISLAND SURRENDERED TO HIM. AIRMAN WHO MADE A FORCED LANDING

Sergeant Pilot Sydney Cohen, who received the surrender of the Italian island of Lampedusa when his plane, through lack of fuel, was forced to land, was a tailor's cutter at Simpson's factory in Stoke Newington-road before he joined the R.A.F three and a half years ago. His home address is at 42 Mildenhall-road . . . where his sister, Mrs Lily Collins, has been 'besieged' with callers since the news was announced of Cohen's adventure.

Cohen's former family home had been in Coronation Gardens, though his parents died before the devastating bombing raid.

While piloting a Swordfish aircraft engaged on sea rescue work, Cohen, with two other members of the crew, had to make a forced landing on Lampedusa . . . he said that as they came down he saw a burnt hangar and burnt aircraft all around.

The white sheets were waved at them by people on the edge of the airfield, and two Italian officers came over, followed by civilians.

The British airmen demanded to see the commander of the island and he received them in a crowded office.

Suddenly everyone made a dash for shelter, although there was no sound of gunfire. They joined the Italian commander in an operations room 75 feet below ground level, and he insisted on giving Sergeant Pilot Cohen a scrap of paper with his signature on it.

'He asked us to take the scrap of paper to Malta and explain to the authorities that the island of Lampedusa had surrendered' added Cohen. Meanwhile Allied planes were continuing the strafing.

Cohen flew instead to Tunis and reported what had happened. He still retains the 'surrender document' and has been nicknamed by his crew-mates 'The King of Lampedusa'.

During both conflicts local people raised funds for the war effort. One such was organized by L.F. James, superintendent of Hackney Baths, and featured in the Hackney Gazette *on 27 March 1942:*

HACKNEY'S WARSHIP EFFORT GOES SWIMMINGLY. GALA AT PUBLIC BATHS
A model of Hackney's destroyer Racehorse – the work of the staff at the Hackney Central Baths . . . was 'under fire' there on Wednesday night.

The occasion was a swimming gala promoted by . . . L.F. James . . . The Mayor (Councillor W. Nichols) . . . concluded [his] speech . . . by inviting the spectators to bombard the Racehorse to see if they could sink her.

A model battleship at Hackney Baths, possibly during 'Wings for Victory' week in March 1943.

The float model of HMS *Thrasher* all ready for 'Warship Week', March 1942.

The boat, with smoke pouring from its funnel, glided majestically along the water and scores of silver and bronze coins were aimed at her. There were several direct hits, but the Racehorse weathered the showers of metal and yielded a respectable sum for Warship Week.

Total Hackney funds for the week reached £407,000. Other events included water polo and a mock dispute between a policeman and policewoman posing as man and wife, which ended up as a fight in the water. A third policeman intervened but had to be rescued by the woman. Not to be outdone, Shoreditch went below the waves for 'Warship Week'. This piece came from the Hackney Gazette *for 23 March 1942:*

MODEL SUBMARINE AT SHOREDITCH
This week a model submarine will tour Shoreditch streets and an attractive list of events has been arranged.

Each day at 3pm a savings 'thermometer' outside the Town Hall, Old-street, will be ceremoniously changed – today Miss Polly Ward, the well known actress will officiate.

Other events included whist drives, a concern by the G-Esters and a march of the armed forces down Hackney-road and along Old-street.

Shoreditch suffered considerably from bombing. The Hackney Gazette *published a report from the borough librarian on 23 February 1942 in advance of the re-opening of the Hoxton Library in Pitfield Street on 2 March. It had stayed open despite minor damage until April 1941 when a large bomb in the garden opposite forced it to close. An emergency lending service was revived but ceased two weeks later when a direct hit by incendiaries and high explosives left it unsafe. Haggerston Library on Kingsland Road had lost its glass roof and windows in September 1940, but re-opened in April 1941.*

Businesses also had a tough time. The tobacco firm of R. & J. Hill lost their premises on the west side of Shoreditch High Street in the blitz of 1941. To indicate their determination to remain in business and in the area, the Hackney Gazette *of 25 September 1942 reported on the erection of the Spinet House Pavilion on the site, and the chairman promised a parcel of cigarettes would be sent to every Shoreditch prisoner of war.*

But the major problem was housing. On 20 October 1944 the Hackney Gazette *reported on the deliberations of Shoreditch Council's Reconstruction Committee. There were three ways in which the problem of housing could be met:*

First by repairing property which was not too badly damaged. The Borough Surveyor had already proceeded with these first aid repairs. Secondly they could adapt existing property [although] practically all the property in Shoreditch was worn out, but on account of the extreme hardship undergone by homeless families, they had picked out a few of the best properties and were adapting them according to the suggestions laid down by the Ministry of Health. The third method was to provide the homeless with temporary huts. . . . [I]f the Council decided to erect Portal houses they would have these houses for ten years, but they hoped long before ten years they would be able to build permanent houses.

In the event Shoreditch got 115 of what one councillor called 'modest bungalows' and by November 1944 had started to erect them on sites in Whiston Road and Weymouth Terrace. The press suggested that they also go up on the ruined churchyard of St Mary's

Portal housing, Whiston Street, *c.* 1950. The war-damaged St Stephen's Church in Haggerston is seen in the background.

Church, Haggerston, which presented a desolate site after the bombing of 1940 that had destroyed the church:

The ground was rain sodden, depressing looking and littered with rubbish, a scene of desolation and neglect. The top of the shattered drinking fountain – the inscription still upon it – lay a considerable distance from the base, and heaps of masonry, dead leaves, pieces of old iron, bricks and stones, tin cans and fallen tree trunks left a dismal impression on the mind.

The churchyard later became an open space in a postwar housing development.

The advent of V1 and V2 rockets in 1944/5 brought back the threat of death to local people. This brief notice appeared in the Hackney Gazette *of 2 March 1945 after an incident at Whiston Road gas works.*

ROCKET FALLS ON GASOMETER

When a V-bomb fell on a gasometer in Southern England recently, the day shift were taking over from the employees on night duty. The rocket completely destroyed the gasometer, releasing over two million cubic feet of gas, which belched into the sky with a vivid yellow flame.

A street party in Daubeney Road to celebrate victory over Japan (VJ Day), 1945.

Fortunately there were no fatal casualties, but several employees were taken to hospital suffering from injuries due to flying metal, bricks and glass. Several workshops were badly damaged.

Forty local people were also hurt and the doors and windows of the adjoining school were blown out, but there were no children there at the time.

By the end of the war in Europe, 736 people from Hackney had been killed and 2,303 injured. In late May the Hackney Gazette *reported on the capture of Lord Haw Haw, William Joyce, remembered locally as a Fascist candidate in the LCC election in Shoreditch in 1934. Shoreditch's MP Ernest Thurtle had not forgotten – he received an anonymous letter asking for Joyce to be returned to Shoreditch and placed in the local stocks, although the Gazette of 11 May 1945 had been unable to support the sort of punishment that had been handed out to Mussolini.*

On 11 May 1945 the Hackney Gazette *reported on the official celebrations for VE Day, which included bonfires on almost every bomb site and crowds out on Mare Street, Kingsland Road and Stoke Newington High Street. Further peace celebrations followed on VJ day in August 1945, when Japan surrendered. Shoreditch celebrations were muted with a band playing on Geffrye Gardens and a thanksgiving service at St John's Church, Hoxton. The finale of the end of war celebrations was the victory parade held through east London in June 1946. Part of the route included Old Street, and the crowds and civic dignitaries were able to see the cavalcade pass.*

By the mid-1950s a nuclear war was regarded as a possible threat that needed to be planned for. The Hackney Gazette *of 22 June 1956 carried this piece:*

HACKNEY IN H-BOMB FILM. FOUR-YEARS-OLD STAR OF GRIM STORY
Four-years-old Jill Payton of Queensdown-road, Clapton, members of Hackney's W.V.S., Civil Defence Corps and the borough itself are all frighteningly convincing in a Home Office film shot in and around Hackney that shows what happens when an H-bomb explodes.

Jill, who is the granddaughter of the local W.V.S. organiser, Mrs Elizabeth Garrett, is shown in some of the film's grimmest scenes, trapped and crying in debris after the bomb has gone off.

Members of the W.V.S appear as people left homeless in the wake of the tremendous explosion, with C.D. members acting as rescue parties and casualties in the sequences made at Bully Fen, Hackney's C.D. training ground.

TEARS STRATEGY
Cartoons are used to show the effect of the bomb's heat flash many miles away, but the final scenes with Jill will probably be the one that sticks in people's minds.

When the film was being made, Jill crawled around happily in the rubble for the makers, R.H.R. Productions, but the difficulty was to make her cry convincingly. Mrs Garrett solved that by walking away as though she was leaving the child, who promptly burst into tears while the cameras recorded her genuine emotion.

The film is called simply The H-Bomb and was produced for the Home Office to be used for training purposes. Among those who helped in its production were Hackney Council, Civil Defence Corps, W.V.S, police and L.C.C.

An advert that appeared in the *Hackney Gazette*, 18 May 1953.

The Home Office have decided that the film may be shown on television and a copy is being considered for use by the B.B.C.

Earlier, on 11 May 1953, the Hackney Gazette *had inspected a model of what was presumed would be the likely effects of an A-bomb falling on Hackney, with the aid of a map of Hackney and models at the Civil Defence centre on Mare Street. A wartime blitz was recreated in December 1954 on Hackney Marshes, with made-up casualties hidden among pre-arranged rubble. Ambulances went into action and plenty of hot soup was made on emergency cookers. Another civil defence demonstration reported on 25 October 1954 included a jet bomber flying over the Town Hall, 'bombs' being dropped on the roof and three 'casualties' staggering out, while a fourth was lowered 60 ft to the ground from the roof.*

Not all local people were convinced by the government film and the Mayor, local clergy and other citizens took part in a 4-mile bomb protest march through north-east London on 27 June 1957. The march, organized by the Hackney Committee for the Abolition of Nuclear Weapon Tests, delivered a petition to Parliament signed by 10,000 people and ended in Montague Place, Holborn, with a short meeting.

CHAPTER EIGHT

RELIGION, RACE AND POLITICS

WOMEN

For many women marriage ended their working careers in the early part of the twentieth century. There was a small debate on this topic in the letters column of the Hackney Gazette *in September 1902:*

'SHOULD WOMEN WORK?'
Sir, – Yes; more so when the husband's funds are low and cannot keep her or give her the necessaries of life. For my part, I should be much happier if I were earning my own living. Independence is a great thing.

I am gifted and accomplished in many ways, but am prevented from fulfilling these gifts on account of the dislike and jealousy of my husband, so the monotonous life of domestic work has to go on without a break into the pleasures which my mind and brain are working to get at. Can nothing be done for such a woman?

A married woman

8 September 1902
Sir – In answer to 'A Married Woman', who writes on the above subject in today's issue, my opinion is that no wife should work if the husband is able and willing to keep her; but what is meant by the necessaries of life is probably in this case a matter of opinion. Your correspondent says 'independence is a great thing', but there is no person more independent than a good wife who is dependant on her husband if the woman is a good manager.

May I suggest to 'A Married Woman', that she should read 'Katherine Regina' by the late Sir Walter Besant. The description in that book of the troubles of a single young woman who found it difficult to get a living is no fancy picture. There are many of them in real life, who, like a girl of eighteen the author represents, may say, 'Never enough money, food or dress, and never any society at all'. And there are many among the poorest class of women, who, like the one described in . . . [the] 'Song of the Shirt', have reason to say of death – 'I scarcely feel his terrible shape, it seems so like my own.'

Those of us who are (like your correspondent) gifted and accomplished in many ways, must surely have resources within ourselves to comfort us for the monotonous round of domestic work of which she complains, and by contrasting our lot with the hundreds less fortunate we shall probably all agree that we have much to be thankful for, and that we ought to be 'happy though married'.

E.M.B.

Maude Lucas, 1925.

Unmarried women might have a career, but there were strict limitations to it. In June 1925 Miss Maude Kathleen Lucas of 96 Herbert Street, off New North Road, was placed third in the Daily Graphic *Colleen Moore Competition, in which prizes were offered for short essays submitted by ambitious women and girls. A welfare worker who served on several Shoreditch committees, Lucas, then aged fifty-nine, continued to hope that she would be able to enter Parliament:*

'I think the competition is the chance of a life-time', she said. 'Every woman is now ambitious and should be given the chance to show that ambition. Mine is to relieve the squalor of the slums. I have lived for some years in the slums of Shoreditch and Hoxton and have worked among the people, especially children. My set purpose was to study the conditions and social problems of their life first hand. There is so much, so very much to be done, and I feel keenly that it is up to every member of the community to put his or her whole weight and ability on the side that shall counteract Communism and the revolutionary menace, which is gaining ground and being propagated in a far greater degree than is generally known. The trouble needs the regeneration of the workers by loving and understanding sympathy, by tireless teaching, leading and educating, and by helping them in their difficulties'.

The Daily Graphic *added that Lucas lived in a single room in Hoxton with no hobbies other than her garden and books. But as with many other dedicated women, her ambition was not to be realized.*

RACE AND IMMIGRATION

The Hackney area has been home to people from other countries since at least the sixteenth century and has had a Jewish population since the late seventeenth century. But newspaper evidence of a black community in the area before 1945 is slender. There were visits from entertainers and the famous – for example in September 1876 the 87-year-old Revd Josiah Henson, a black preacher who was said to be the character on whom Harriet Beecher Stowe's Uncle Tom was based, travelled over from the USA and gave addresses at Mildmay Park Conference Hall and Trinity Congregational Church, Walford Road.

The 1880s had seen large-scale Jewish immigration into east London. This is part of an editorial that appeared in the Hackney & Kingsland Gazette *of 28 May 1902:*

The question of alien immigration and its restriction has been before the public a great deal of late, and there can be no denying the fact that in the East End at any rate, the problem is very acute. It has forced up the rents of houses to abnormal proportions and caused considerable overcrowding, with a correspondingly detrimental effect on health and morals. Of course the majority of these aliens are foreign Jews from Russia and Poland, and there is also the German variety. But objection is taken not so much to their nationality as to the condition in which they arrive. Absolutely penniless is perhaps the best description of these persons when they reach our hospitable shores – here to swell the ranks of the great army of unemployed and to force wages down to starvation level. Some light was thrown on the question of cheap alien labour at the sitting yesterday of the Royal Commission which is investigating this matter. A member of the boot industry, which is so extensively carried out in Hackney and Bethnal Green, declared that the trade has been declining for some years until it is now in so bad a condition as it can possibly be owing to the influx of destitute immigrants. It is characteristic of the alien workman that he never learns a trade thoroughly, but after securing employment in a certain branch of it, becomes to an extent an expert and is able to keep a fully qualified man out. He works cheaper and generally under conditions to which no English workman would submit. . . .

Even to the point where new trousers at 1s 9d were cheaper than a second-hand pair!

In the 1906 general election the issue of the employment of Chinese labour in the Transvaal spilled over into fears of immigrant labour coming into Britain. In Walthamstow there were pro- and anti-Chinese parties (respectively the Conservatives and the Radicals). In Hoxton Radical candidate Henry Ward went one stage further and employed an actor costumed as a travesty of a Chinese man to support his message.

Suffragettes proclaiming the cause of votes for women in the general election campaign in the Haggerston ward, July 1908.

By the mid-1950s there had been significant immigration from the West Indies into Hackney. In March 1955 a local paper reported that Hackney Methodists had allowed a black American evangelist, Bishop J.E. Watley, to use the mission hall in Richmond Road as a centre for a religious revival for black people in the area. Watley, who modelled himself on Billy Graham, also preached on local market streets. Traditional churches were having problems attracting black congregations. In the Stoke Newington Observer of 5 April 1957, the vicar of St Andrew's, Bethune Road, said that although his church included members from the West Indies, Central Africa, Nigeria and Ghana, they constituted relatively few of the new arrivals, who were from countries with a high record of church attendance. He was to hold a weekend school to address the issue. In the same year the Hackney Gazette of 20 December reported on a Sunday school held by the Hackney and Stoke Newington Labour Party on 'The problem of colonial immigration'.

One of Hackney's first black politicians was Dr David Pitt, who was elected as a Labour candidate to Stoke Newington's London County Council seat in April 1961. Pitt, then aged forty-seven, was born in Grenada and had founded the West Indian National Party, been a councillor in a Trinidad borough council and stood as a parliamentary candidate in Hampstead in the 1959 general election. Pitt went on to be a GLC member for Hackney and chairman of the Campaign Against Racial Discrimination. He became the second West Indian peer in 1975.

In 1961 the commissioner for the West Indies, British Guiana and British Honduras presented the annual prizes at Colvestone Primary School, though he was disappointed at the relatively small number of West Indian parents attending. The headmaster said that there had been a considerable increase in West Indian pupils in the last three years – before then there had been very few. He had anticipated problems but,

The West Indian children were accepted by the others immediately and he hoped that more of them would come in the future.

However, things were not easy for black people. The Stoke Newington Observer of 17 December 1965 reported on a Hackney Council survey:

Only 10.8% of 400 coloured immigrants interviewed in a Hackney Borough Council survey last month said colour prejudice was the problem that bothered them most. More than four times as many said housing was their main difficulty, while 8% felt that employment was their trouble.

David Pitt being congratulated by David Weitzman, Labour MP for Stoke Newington, after his election victory, April 1961.

Other significant statistics included only 27% intended to stay permanently in the U.K. 71% did not vote in elections, 40% did not attend social gatherings where there were whites present and 76% were unaware that Hackney had a specially appointed officer for 'non white residents'. Of the 407 people out of 500 who completed the form, 61% were aged between 21 and 35, only 3% were professional people and the majority had come over between 1959 and 1962.

The survey took place against the national background of a government white paper, 'Immigration from the Commonwealth'. Hackney had taken a lead in community relations, having established a local council, the Hackney Council for the Welfare of Coloured Citizens, in 1959 and appointed the first ever officer whose principal concern was immigrant welfare – even if they had not provided enough publicity for the initiative. Consequently there was a fierce debate when one Council member voted against the motion to urge the government not to take up the restrictive proposals in the white paper – and urged that all immigration be banned for five years.

Hackney Council continued to take positive initiatives for ethnic minority communities. This report appeared in the Hackney Gazette *on 4 September 1981.*

A West Indian variety concert at Brooke House School, February 1965. The concert was organized by Hackney Council and the North London West Indian Association.

YOUNG PROBLEM BLACKS TO STAY IN HACKNEY

Hackney Council is to introduce a revolutionary new scheme for West Indian problem youngsters and their families. Instead of putting difficult children into care, and sending them off to residential homes outside the borough, they will arrange for them to be looked after by fellow West Indians in Hackney.

The aim of this unique proposal – the first of its kind in London – is to keep black youngsters in the community and where possible to keep them living at home.

An initial placement of ten children was to be sent to Caribbean House, home of the Hoxton based West Indian Concern. The scheme was intended to be cheaper to run and would avoid the aggravation of problems for the children arising from social workers not having enough knowledge of West Indian culture.

Race relations on Hackney's Council estates were the subject of a survey in 1982, when it was reported that the Asian community, making up only 4% of the Council's tenants, were making nearly one-third of complaints of racial harassment, with just under another third coming from the black community, from a total of fifteen reported cases in the previous twelve months.

But it was the relationship of the black community with the police that was causing rising concern. On 12 January 1983 Colin Roach, a black man, was found with a fatal shot-gun wound just inside the door of Stoke Newington police station. The police claim that he had killed himself was disputed by his family and there were many in the black community who believed that he had been murdered. Feelings ran high. This report is from the Hackney Gazette *on 25 January 1983:*

A demonstration outside Stoke Newington police station after the death of Colin Roach, January 1983.

Fighting and looting on Saturday marred what had been a peaceful protest demanding an inquiry on Colin Roach, who died from a shot gun blast at Stoke Newington police station.

Twenty-two people were arrested on charges including threatening behaviour and obstruction. . . . Some 300 marchers left Hackney Town hall at 1pm and went to [Stoke Newington] police station. . . . After observing a two minute silence in remembrance of Mr Roach, the protestors left for a rally at Stoke Newington common. Trouble started as the gathering dispersed. About 150 people ran from the common down the middle of Stoke Newington High Street towards the police station.

Traffic came to a halt as police officers formed a cordon outside the station and across the road. The police say the charging crowd ran into the cordons. With beer cans flying and shoppers taking shelter in doorways, scuffles broke out and a number of arrests were made.

A jeweller's shop in Northwold Road was looted at the same time. Four Hackney councillors who were on the march later complained to police about their rough handling of demonstrators and racist remarks. The event had been the third demonstration since Roach's death, and there were to be several more in ensuing months.

The 1930s saw the rise of the British Union of Fascists. In November 1936 there were protests when Hackney Council let King's Hall, at Hackney Baths, to the British Union of Fascists.

An attempt to rescue a colleague from arrest at the Communist meeting in Ridley Road, August 1947.

Oswald Mosley on the back of a lorry at Ridley Road, August 1962.

The Labour Party considered that a previous ban by the Conservatives on the use of the hall by the Communists was wrong, and they felt that they did not have the right to censor lettings, especially as undertakings had been given that the Fascists would not march to the hall.

But there was trouble at a Labour meeting at Hackney Town Hall in March 1939, when 200 Fascists were present and in the same month Fascists broke up a meeting organized by the local Ambulance for Spain Committee at Shoreditch Town Hall. Speakers included the Shoreditch MP Ernest Thurtle and Professor J.B.S. Haldane, but the speeches were constantly interrupted. Fireworks were let off in all parts of the hall, the Fascists sang the Horst Wessel song and chanted 'We want Mosley'. At the close of the meeting police had to rescue Haldane from a group of Fascists bent on attacking him.

Nor did the end of the Second World War see the end of local Fascism. Indeed, the problems in Hackney became worse as rival meetings were organized by Communists. On 31 August the Communists arrived first at Ridley Road in advance of a meeting of the extreme right-wing British League of ex-Service Men. National and local papers reported events differently, but the

League meeting moved to John Campbell Road. Both sides tried to heckle their opponents' meetings, though the League members marched through the streets round Dalston. Two arrests were made and it took over 300 police to restore the peace.

Hackney Council finally banned Fascists from using Council premises in January 1948. However, not all Fascists got off scot free as a result of their activities – one came up before Old Street Magistrate Court charged with chalking the Fascist symbol and 'Hail Mosley' on the wall of a caretaker's hut in Buttesland Street. The magistrate asked the constable to repeat the remark, as he claimed he thought he had heard 'Hell Mosley', and having had his bit of fun fined the offender a pound. In May 1948 Sir Oswald Mosley himself spoke at a Union Movement meeting at Hertford Road. This is part of the report that appeared in a local paper of 3 May:

Strategic action by the police frustrated the hopes of rowdy elements to start disturbances at Sir Oswald Mosley's . . . meeting at Hertford-road, Dalston, on Saturday afternoon. Some twenty minutes after the meeting opened more than a dozen mounted police forced their way through and split the crowd in front of the platform. Yard by yard they cleared everyone from Hertford-road except for two or three hundred of Mosley's own supporters gathered close up to his rostrum.

The police also cleared Stamford and Englefield roads, which reduced the large crowd effect that Mosley had hoped for:

. . . [I]t was raining heavily when Mosley arrived at the Englefield-road end of Hertford-road. He sat in the back of the car, shielded by several of his followers. As the vehicle stopped, he leapt out, climbed on top of the rostrum and stood hatless and without an overcoat as his followers roared their applause and raised their hands in the Fascist salute.

There was still enough of a crowd beyond the police barriers to drown out the loudspeakers carrying Mosley's speech and after 45 minutes he left for an illegal march set to start from

Police hold back demonstrators at the same rally, August 1962. Crowds broke through lines manned by over 300 police and stormed Mosley's lorry.

Highbury. Again 400 police had been required and Mosley's platform had had to have a police guard on it overnight.

In the 1956 Shoreditch Council election twenty-one Fascist candidates stood and focused on a matter obviously close to their hearts. This report comes from the Hackney Gazette *of 9 May 1956.*

RATS ARE ELECTION EVE ISSUE

Bitterest fighting in the local Borough Council elections has been at Shoreditch, between the Socialists, who have 100% control of the retiring council, and Sir Oswald Mosley's 21 Blackshirt candidates. Yesterday Councillor Mrs D. Thurtle, leader of Shoreditch Council, made the following statement to the Gazette in answer to Blackshirt allegations about 'a plague of rats in Whitecross-place.'

'My attention has been drawn to a scurrilous leaflet which has been issued by the Blackshirt Movement in which it is alleged that Whitecross-place . . . is plagued by rats and that the Borough Council have taken no action to deal with these pests. This statement is completely untrue, and in fact for some time past the Public Health Department have carried out a large number of visits of inspection to these flats and a great deal of time has been spent in endeavouring to eradicate the rat nuisance. Every week the Council's sanitary inspectors and rodent staff have worked long hours in suppressing these vermin. In this work the best co-operation has been received from the owners of the property, British Railways. In this connection the sewers adjoining Whitecross-place have also received a good deal of attention . . . [and] the rat infestation has practically ceased.'

Racist slogans against Jews and swastikas were daubed on Walford Road synagogue in January 1960, as reported in the Stoke Newington Observer *for 8 January. The same page of that issue also carried a report on white supremacists' slogans being daubed on walls in Stoke Newington. In July 1962 the newly formed North and East London Co-ordinating Committee of Anti-Fascists held a big meeting at Hackney Town Hall, calling for legislation to make incitement of racial and religious hatred a criminal offence. Many of those attending wore yellow star badges, symbolizing the Yellow Star Movement, another group founded by local vicar Bill Sargent, who spoke at the meeting, saying that 'East London was not the doormat on which the Fascists can wipe their dirty feet.' A further large open-air meeting of the movement was held in Ridley Road the following Sunday.*

A Mosley meeting in Ridley Road in July lead to protesters being injured, including a former Mayor of Hackney, Alderman Louis Sherman, and his wife, and to councillors complaining of police mishandling of the demonstrators. So a further Mosley meeting planned for the first Sunday in September 1962 was likely to have been the focus of even more trouble than usual. The Mayor of Hackney was told twice that the Metropolitan Police had no power to ban it, but shortly before the march was due to take place a deputation from Hackney Council to the Home Office was successful and the police were told to enforce an 1839 act cancelling the meeting.

The end of Mosley's party did not lead to the disappearance of the far right. In the 1970s the National Front had its headquarters in Great Eastern Street and there were some nasty local incidents, including the fire bombing of an Asian family's house in London

Michael Cliffe, Labour MP for Shoreditch and Finsbury, addresses a meeting of the Yellow Star Movement, Ridley Road, September 1962.

Fields in 1980. This resulted in the family being protected by night watches from East London Workers Against Racism and the Hackney Asian Association until Hackney Council was able to re-house them. In October 1980 Hackney Council was finally successful in winning its case to evict the National Front on the ground that they did not have planning permission to use their club building as an office and headquarters. The eviction took place in early December 1980.

In 1937 the Salvation Army offered a temporary home to refugee Basque children, displaced by the Spanish Civil War. But there were some problems between the Army and the children, as this report from the Hackney Gazette *of 31 May 1937 records.*

BASQUE REFUGEE CHILDREN AT CLAPTON
Lack of discipline among 400 Basque refugees now being cared for by the Salvation Army at the Congress hall, Linscott-road, Clapton, is causing difficulties for the

General Evangeline Booth with some of the Basque children at Congress Hall, May 1937.

officers in charge of the children. . . . [T]hese little victims of the Spanish civil War – the first contingent to leave the refugee camp at Stoneham, Hants – were given a warm-hearted reception when they arrived in Hackney last Wednesday by hundreds of women and children, who had waited several hours notwithstanding the rain and a thunderstorm.

They were met at the gates of the Congress Hall by General Evangeline Booth and representatives of the Spanish Embassy and the Basque Government.

The children have soon recovered their natural high spirits, now that the horrors of the Bilbao war front are far behind them and they are proving a lively little crowd to manage. Brigadier J. Martin, who is supervising the arrangements for them, said in an interview with the Gazette on Saturday: 'The youngsters are not settling down too badly, but the girls are much better than the boys. The trouble is that these children have had no schooling since the war started and they are completely undisciplined. The boys go climbing over the walls and roofs like little monkeys. For the most part they have no sense of religion and no use for the Church. They seem to have Communist sentiments.'

Local people were asked not to encourage the children to go out over the low wall on Almack Road and bring any presents to the gatekeeper. And top of the Brigadier's wish list were three or four blackboards, some easels and some exercise books so that schooling could start forthwith.

The 1950 general election saw the emergence of a new party in Stoke Newington. This report on a long lost cause comes from the Stoke Newington Observer *of 13 January 1950.*

'GREENSHIRT' TO FIGHT THE ELECTION
Simultaneously with the release of the official news that the general election would take place on February 23, it was announced that Mr John Hargrave, founder and

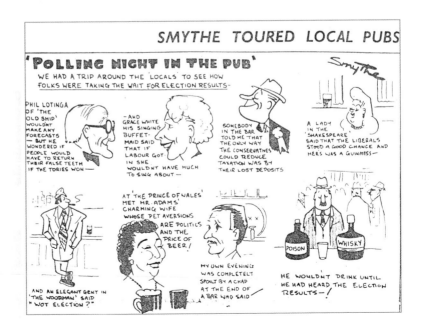

A cartoon by Smythe for the general election, March 1950.

leader of the Social Credit Party – known as the 'Greenshirts' – intended to seek election as a Social Credit candidate in Stoke Newington and Hackney North. This will mean at least a four-cornered fight in the constituency, as there are already three candidates in the field. They are David Weitzman, Labour M.P. for Stoke Newington, Mr W.H. Bishop, Conservative, . . . and Mr Philip Phillips, . . . Liberal. In 1945 Stoke Newington and Hackney returned four MPs – all Labour – but owing to the boundary changes there will be only two in this election. . . .

Both Labour and Conservative candidates expressed curiosity as to how their Greenshirt opponent was funded and why he had chosen Stoke Newington.

Fifty-five-year-old John Hargrave founded the Social Credit Party in 1935 to establish a 'sane economic system' and in 1936–7 he was economic adviser to the Government of Alberta, where the party gained power and has held it ever since. The party founded a North London branch three months ago.

The Observer *added that the only Social Credit candidate ever to contest a British election previously did so at Leeds in 1935 and lost his deposit. Hargrave did not break the mould at Stoke Newington and Weitzman was duly elected.*

Politics was well mixed with religion in late nineteenth-century Hoxton, as one journalist found when he visited socialist parson Cartmel Robinson, Vicar of Holy Trinity. At 6 ft 4 in, Robinson must have towered over many of his parishioners. As he took his visitor on a tour of his parish, they passed a thin boy who was shortly to be sent to a home in Margate. Then,

J. Cartmel Robinson, Vicar of Holy Trinity from 1891 until 1905. He died in 1935, aged eighty-one.

We passed through more shadowed streets and down some steps, and then between two high walls, where we had to walk in single file, until a sharp dive to the right landed us in the backyards of a pile of mean tenements. 'It was somewhere hereabouts,' said my guide 'where I found a dead child lying on the only bed of a one-roomed house. I asked where they put the body when the family used the bed at night and I learnt it was placed until morning upon the only shelf in the house, where they kept the food'.

Robinson believed that London life restricted physical ability and this in turn impeded chances of employment. The answer was play and games. Robinson had also founded a workmen's club a little distance from the church and there was a boys' brigade associated with the church,

... which wears Highland costume. See them, with their drum and fife band passing through the streets and all Hoxton turns out of doors to do honour to them! The London boy as a Highlander needs to be seen to be appreciated. For the elder lads there is a Boys' Guild. Mrs Robinson takes the girls in hand. They, too, have a flourishing guild, of which nearly all the members are working girls. Both Mr and Mrs Robinson believe in bringing the boys and girls into each other's company as much as possible and they hold dances periodically, on the lawn in summer and at the club in winter.

Members of the Hoxton Boys' Brigade dressed in their Highland costume in the grounds of Holy Trinity Vicarage, 1896.

The lawn was part of the vicarage garden and was the scene of waltzes, quadrilles, garden parties and pastoral plays. For the youngest children there were 'Bands of Busy Bees', which included making clothes for the poor.

Robinson was also a member of the Shoreditch Board of Guardians, but felt that the Progressives, supposedly in favour of action for the working classes, did not implement their programmes once in office and would not pay trade-union wages. The mixture would have met the approval of William Morris, even down to the full-scale celebration of May Day in 1901, when a May Pole was put up in the Tower Hamlets Drill Hall in Shaftsbury Street, and Gertie Pearce as Queen of the May paraded through the streets with a costumed escort of Robin Hood, Friar Tuck and his band, monks, sailors, fisher-girls, jesters, soldiers and Vikings. Local people joined in with flags and decorations from their houses and although the association of a fictional romantic rural past with the grim realities of an area the national press had firmly associated with hooliganism in the previous January must have seemed strange then, as it does now, the money raised from the event was used to provide holidays for the local children.

Church services come in a variety of shapes and sizes. This report appeared in the Hackney Gazette *of 29 April 1953:*

Brought Washing Machine for Blessing

A tall white washing machine and large white gas stove were conspicuous objects near the altar of the Parish Church of St John at Hackney on Sunday morning. Their presence there, with many other goods normally exhibited in shops and showrooms, symbolised the observance of Industrial Sunday. The goods were there for blessing and as offerings of 'labour and service to Almighty God'.

Among the offerings were bricks, cement, trowels, saws and other tools, a fireside chair, clothing and fountain pens. No such display of tools and products of local industry has ever before been made in the Parish Church of Hackney, so far as the

The Revd Ambrose Wright outside the Round Chapel, December 1975.

senior member of the congregation can remember, but the new custom for Industrial Sunday, now auspiciously inaugurated, is likely to be continued and may well develop in scope as the years go on. . . .

While the body of the church was nearly half full, some disappointment was felt by the organisers of this special service that it had not attracted a larger attendance of those directly concerned with Hackney's industrial life. At the same time it was felt that a good beginning to a fuller and more representative observance of Industrial Sunday in the borough had been made.

More typical was this report from the Hackney Gazette *of 9 December 1975 on the problems faced by Anglican and Nonconformist churches of falling rolls and buildings that were ageing and expensive to maintain.*

A row is brewing about the future of one of Hackney's finest buildings, – Clapton Park United Reformed Church. The Round Chapel, as it is known locally, was built in 1871 in Lower Clapton Road and has been listed as being of great architectural and historical value. But it has become a millstone round the neck of the church's governing body – they simply cannot afford to run such a huge building. Heating bills . . . are said to be enormous and the woodwork has to be treated for dry rot.

The church elders want to demolish the building and then construct a smaller church and church hall. At the side of the church would be two blocks containing some 22 flats.

There was local opposition to the planning application. In the article the minister would have liked to have seen the chapel converted to an arts centre, while the Hackney Society wanted it to be used as a public amenity centre. The problem proved a difficult one for all parties to resolve and a solution was not found for nearly another twenty years, when the church was transferred to the Hackney Historic Buildings Trust, created by people active in the Hackney Society, who were able to secure funding for the necessary repairs and explore using the building for musical events.

CHAPTER NINE

SOCIAL ATTITUDES AND ENTERTAINMENT

As well as a full-size theatre, Shoreditch was home to the famous Pollock's Toy Theatre Shop at 73 Hoxton Street. These extracts come not from a local paper, but from an article that appeared in John O'London's Weekly *for 30 October 1936.*

In you are a connoisseur of experiences . . . you may collect a rare one, only a penny tram ride from Holborn Bars. Turn up narrow Hoxton Street and proceed . . . until you come to No 73. Look closely or you will miss it, for it seems to aim at the inconspicuous, as if shrinking away from the unseemly racket that hems it in. The owner's name is indecipherable. It has not been regilded these forty years.

Behind the square-paned windows, a brilliant coloured toy theatre with wings seven deep surmounts a dusty sea of pencils, buttons, spectacle cases, marbles, knitting-needles and farthing sweets. The door window is full of coloured prints of theatrical scenes and characters of a vanished time.

As you push the door, a bell rings at the back and through a glass partition you see a very old man with a handsome and distinguished bearing rising from his chair by the fire and enter the shop. He is none other than Mr Benjamin Pollock, last of the toy theatre makers. . . . More than sixty years ago he took this shop over from his father-in-law, Redington, an earlier manufacturer of the Victorian juvenile drama.

Pollock's shop. From a painting by Charles Ivanhoe, 1937. The fifteen-year-old girl who posed for the artist had been sent out by her family to buy potatoes and was scolded for being away so long!

This is your moment, you may lean on the time-mellowed oak counter and buy a Penny Plain or Tuppence Coloured exactly as the young Dickens bought them here, and as thousands of grown-ups and children have bought them for over a century.

Famous visitors also included Robert Louis Stevenson, Bulwer-Lytton, Baron Rothschild, Ellen Terry, G.K. Chesterton, Winston Churchill, Charlie Chaplin and many others. But the business was on the verge of closing as Benjamin was no longer able to carry on the printing. His two daughters, Louisa and Susan, both born on the premises, had stayed on and worked with their father:

Susan of the sensitive fingers used to cut out the scenes and characters from the sheets as her father printed them. The average play took her a day to do. But the Battle of Waterloo took two days because of the care needed to cut out the horses' bridles and legs.

Louisa did the colouring, sometimes by hand and sometimes with stencils. A single sheet took from five to fifteen stencils . . . her colours of forty years ago as bright as yesterday's. She uses gamboge, carmine, Prussian blue and black, mixing them with her own secret process, with gum and sugar.

The Pollocks' work received additional publicity in an exhibition at the George Inn, Southwark, in November 1936. After Benjamin's death in 1937 Louisa kept the business going and it survived bomb damage to the shop during the Second World War and is shortly to move from its present premises in Scala Street to Greenwich.

Changes in taste and competition from local cinema put pressure on the local theatres. The Shoreditch theatres were in decline from the early twentieth century and had all either closed or been converted to cinemas by the mid-1920s. Further north, Hackney and Stoke Newington each had a Frank Matcham-designed theatre – the Alexandra on Stoke Newington Road, which opened in 1897, and the Hackney Empire on Mare Street, opened in 1901. The Stoke Newington Observer carried a report on nude shows in London theatres on 19 April 1940, interviewing John Robertson, whose 'Strip Please' was showing at a Stoke Newington theatre, presumably the Alexandra. The Lord Chamberlain had just refused to relax a ban on stage nudity, although posed tableaus were to stay. Robertson had made some changes to the act: 'Diane, who is appearing in the show, did dance in the nude, but now we have cut that out and she appears fully clothed'.

Nudity was not enough to save the Alexandra, which, after a postwar revival by a Yiddish theatre group between 1947 and 1949, closed in 1950. Just before it shut down there was further controversy when the play Breach of Marriage transferred there from the West End. With its theme of artificial insemination and test-tube babies, it

In 1955 Ann Black, a Shoreditch factory worker, then aged eighteen, answered an advertisement and became 'Amber', the 'Girl in the Bottle'. She had to sit in her bottle for up to 8 hours a day and travelled all around the country. 'Sailors had had ideas of adding Ann to their collection of ships in bottles. Many have proposed marriage. Ann says "No".'

provoked one outraged Christian to try to enlist local ministers to get the play banned, though the only support the Stoke Newington Observer *could find came from the Catholics.*

Six years after the Alexandra closed, it was the turn of the Hackney Empire. This report comes from the Hackney Gazette *of 8 February 1956:*

HACKNEY EMPIRE'S LAST CURTAIN

. . . [The] second and final performance at the Hackney Empire on Saturday night must have been an unforgettable occasion for the 2,000 people who were there. The packed house, the excitement and the warm affection that flowed between cast and audience recalled the golden days of this famous music hall, but at the final curtain, when the whole theatre rose to sing 'Auld Lang Syne', the sadness of the moment was clear on every face.

Old-timer G.H. Elliot ['*the Chocolate Coloured Coon*' – *white men 'blacking up' were still regarded as acceptable in the media as late as the 1960s*] made the farewell speech. . . . And then welcomed on stage Mrs E. Day, a 71-years-old Clapton lady who was at the Empire when the curtain first went up in 1901.

As TV newsreel cameras filmed the scene from a box, 'G.H.' referred to the Empire's future and said 'I hope you won't lose us all entirely. Although you won't see us in the flesh, I hope you'll be able to see some of us on your TV sets at home from the Hackney Empire stage.' . . .

On Monday the Empire passed into the hands of Associated Television and the Gazette understands that some drastic alterations will be made to the theatre's interior before viewers see the live TV shows that are to be produced there in the future.

Luckily for the Empire no radical work took place before it was sold to become a bingo hall. It re-opened as a live theatre in 1986.

Cinemas did occasionally host live events. In October 1953 the audience of the Regal Cinema, Well Street, saw a performance by the seven women who danced the can-can in the opening sequences of the film Moulin Rouge, *giving 'a fine display of frills and high kicks and got a big ovation from the audience'.*

The heyday of the local cinema in Hackney lasted for little more than ninety years. Two reports capture high noon and sunset. The first is from the Hackney Gazette *for 3 May 1939.*

THE DALSTON ODEON: OPENING OF NEW PICTURE THEATRE

The latest of the great chain of Odeon luxury cinemas stretching through the country, the Dalston Odeon, Stamford-road, was opened with impressive cere-

Cover from the programme of the last production at the Hackney Empire, February 1956.

The Dalston Odeon, 1939.

mony on Monday night by Mr F.C. Watkins, M.P. for Central Hackney. The building, which stands on a triangular site, is an arresting example of the new cinema architecture and with its lofty elevation and facing material of terra cotta, carried out in black and cream above, with a black plinth, its simple but effective treatment takes the eye.

There is seating for over 2,070 persons, and a feature of the auditorium is that an excellent view of the screen is obtainable from every angle, the interior decorations consist of a quiet blending of green peach and gold colours in the modern abstract style.

The band of the 1st Battalion, the Royal Scots, was in attendance at the opening ceremony and regimental pipers greeted the arrival of Mr Watkins with a gay skirl of pipes. . . .

And the second is from the Hackney Gazette *for 3 March 1981.*

THE ODEON STAGES ITS VERY LAST SHOW

The Stamford Hill Odeon is staging its first show for 10 years – it is being demolished. After a decade of neglect the former de luxe picture palace is being levelled to make way for a new development.

A landmark in the north of the borough, the site was to be used for a supermarket, but developers Fairview Estate Ltd were unavailable for comment when contacted on Monday about its future. The Odeon is reputed to have seated 2,000 people in its heyday until it fell victim of the 1960s cinema decline. Unlike the Dalston Odeon, now similarly closed, the giant theatre was never converted into three smaller cinemas.

Despite a 'Save the Odeon' campaign and moves to have Hackney Council take it over as a sports centre, the Stamford Hill site has become increasingly derelict.

A Hackney Council spokesman said it was pleasing to see some action underway to bring the popular corner back into use. Meanwhile the borough fears that plans to convert the Dalston Odeon into a DIY superstore have fallen by the wayside.

The Stamford Hill Odeon, formerly the Regent Cinema, was eventually replaced by a supermarket. The Dalston Odeon was demolished in the mid-1980s and a housing development, which includes flats for older people, stands on the site.

In the early 1950s Hackney Council had grand plans for an open-air civic theatre to celebrate the Festival of Britain. The chosen site would have been the centre of Clapton Square and it would have been linked to the creation of a civic theatre company. However, there were objections, led by the Clapton-square Protection Committee, to the site and to the £17,000 estimated cost. After a tribunal hearing in April 1951, the Minister of Local Government and Planning vetoed the project on economic grounds. A decade later Hackney was able to launch a drama festival. This report comes from the Hackney Gazette *of 5 May 1961:*

ALL SET FOR HACKNEY DRAMA FESTIVAL

Germ of an idea for an amateur drama festival in Hackney came from a suggestion by the Theatre Royal Advisory Council of a Festival at Stratford covering all the neighbouring boroughs. This proposal is still being considered but in the meantime Hackney Borough Council have decided to go ahead independently.

Local drama groups and the LCC's Further Education Service combined and the event was held on 13 May at Brooke House School's theatre. Three short plays were included in an evening programme, and the Gazette *hoped that a comprehensive arts festival might develop from this event. That first festival sold out and the following year the Council launched a more ambitious programme. This report is from the* Hackney Gazette *for 23 March 1962.*

HACKNEY AND THE ARTS. 'WE KNOW HOW TO LIVE' SAYS MAYOR

Hackney Council's arts festival, which ends tomorrow, was given a fine send-off by the Mayor of Hackney (Alderman L. Sherman) before a large crowd. . . . Describing the big response to the Council's initiative in organising the event, the Mayor alluded to a national Sunday newspaper which referring to Hackney's 15-year-old top singer Helen Shapiro, recently stated that she 'came from the insalubrious borough of Hackney'.

'It may well be that our borough is not so nice because of its lack of reportable cases of rape, arson and murder' he declared 'What we do know in East London in general, and . . . Hackney in particular, is how to live and, above all, we want to live better. It is perfectly true that Hackney has no coming-out ball for its young ladies – but it has its family life, which we foster, nurture and sustain. We are not producing any debutantes, but we can produce a playwright or two.'

One of these playwrights is talented Arnold Wesker, who lives in Hackney. He has leant his name to a trophy and will present it to the best drama group.

The Festival week also included an exhibition by the Hackney Photographic Society, with some slides set to music, while the drama included Shakespeare, 'a Midlands comedy and a play by one of the most notable French dramatists'.

There were also local arts initiatives. This report comes from the Hackney Gazette *for 31 December 1981.*

Richard Burton appeared in the film version of John Osborne's play *Look Back in Anger*, released in 1959. Part of the film was shot at Dalston Junction railway station, and Burton was photographed with co-star Mary Ure in the tiny station bar in November 1958. Station staff member Mrs E. Harling is pouring the stout.

A People's Palace That's Chats

If the term 'community centre' conjures up visions of bearded middle class intellectuals spouting Marxist theories on dialectical materialism and earnest unmarried mothers with cropped hair, dungarees and badges proclaiming a commitment to the Women's Movement, the Socialist Workers Party and CND, then Chats' Palace is not a community centre.

But despite an uncharacteristic shortage of trendy lefties, Chats' Palace is precisely that. It provides a forum for local art, drama, pop, cabaret, comedy and a booming music hall revival. It provides work for unemployed youngsters. A recent ten month job creation project gave the place a face lift and gave jobless school leavers from nearby estates their first taste of work. It puts on play schemes to keep kids occupied in the school holidays and it runs workshops aimed at involving everyone in the local community. Walk into the bar any night of the week and . . . [y]ou will see a few groups of local people, old and young, working class and middle class, black and white happily chatting about topics as diverse as football, politics and music over a pint or two of real ale.

Pop into the theatre and you will probably find people enthusiastically rehearsing for a music hall show . . . or going through a reading for a new play. . . .

Built as Homerton Library in 1912, the building closed in 1971 and after a short period as a Citizens' Advice Bureau, was intended to be demolished as part of a traffic scheme. When that was abandoned, a local committee asked Hackney Council to consider converting the building to become an arts centre. It was leased to what then became the Homerton Community Centre Project in 1975 and the first event, the Hackney Marsh Fun Festival barn dance, took place in the summer of 1976. Major building work took place in the late 1970s and by the time of the report, Chats' Palace had become 'one of the best centres for community arts in London', according to Alan Rossiter, project co-ordinator.

Hackney also made its own media appearances. This piece is from the Hackney Gazette *for 15 April 1955.*

BBC Come Down Our Way

An unobtrusive black car, unusual only in the amount of tape recording equipment stacked in the back, travelled round Hackney all Wednesday, gathering material for a programme next Sunday in one of the B.B.C.'s most popular features – 'Down Your Way'. This is the third programme in a new series, and that unobtrusive black car has already been to Crewe and to Elgin, in Scotland.

Hackney was selected, producer Phyllis Robinson told a Gazette reporter, mainly because compere Franklin Englemann knows it well, likes it and suggested it. Both Miss Robinson and he have local connections, so they had personal knowledge of the borough to help them in their job; giving a huge radio audience a cross-section of Hackney people and life.

Work on the show had started weeks before and ten interviewees had been selected.

First on Wednesday's list was Mr Sid Radley, proprietor of the well-known boat service on the River Lea at Clapton. After an informative interview with him, in which he told a little about his long established family business, the unit moved on to a box making firm in Theydon-road.

The noise and bustle of one of Hackney's markets came next when Mr Englemann arrived in Ridley-road for interviews with George Kane and Mac Solomons, then the recording unit went on to Marshall and Ruchon, a firm of pipemakers in Homerton High Street for a chat with manager Mr G.H. Penton and employee Mrs Doris Hull.

By mid-afternoon recordings were being made at Clarnicos the sweet manufacturers; later at Hackney baths where Leyton Orient player Vic Groves was interviewed while he had an aerotone bath; then came Mr Harry Davis, conductor and founder of the well known local banjo, mandolin and guitar orchestra. In the evening there was an interview with John Christie, first manager of the Hackney Empire and finally one with Miss Kitty Howard, who lives at Buccleuch House, Clapton, the flats for single professional women.

At least one Hackney factory also featured in Workers' Playtime, *in the early 1950s, when the BBC broadcast a programme from Clarnico's confectionery factory in Wallis Road, Hackney Wick.*

Betting was legalized in May 1961, and this report from the Hackney Gazette *on 2 May details the impact this change had on a trade previously confined to the shadows.*

'B' FOR BETS DAY

They used to be grocery stores, barbers shops and second hand 'bargain basements' sandwiched among rows of other shops or old houses in Stepney, Bethnal Green, Hoxton or Hackney. Yesterday they branched out under the proud new title of 'Betting Office'.

The betting shops were open for legitimate business and the well known old street-corner bookie, who for years has divided his time between palming those 'two-bobs each way' from housewives and factory workers and keeping a watchful eye open for the policeman, started on his way out.

'With him go some of the colour of betting', said George Dick, whose door at 181 Kingsland Road Shoreditch, was wide open for business soon after 9am yesterday. 'With some people it was not a case of having a bet as much as enjoying the excitement of getting it on,' he added with a chuckle.

The first 'official' customer to enter his place on Monday was an old lady who had a shilling win 'double' twice.

At another bookie's, Stan Barrett of Hoxton Street, where the builders were still at work, the reporter got further comment from Mr Barrett:

The Crown public house, Shoreditch, was a haunt of bird fanciers who held bird-singing contests there. Members are listening to one contest with Mr Harvey, the judge, on the right, 1950.

He does not agree with other bookmakers who think that only a third of the offices opening that day would survive the year. 'Of course overheads are high' he admitted. 'But like every new business, there are bound to be expenses at the beginning. I think the idea of betting shops is a great improvement. The punter does not have to chase the bookie's runner all round the streets as the runner is being chased by the police.' . . .

Nearly all agreed that it was sad in many respects. 'The street bookie has long been regarded in the East End as something of an institution' said a burly Stepney bookie (all his life in the business). Said one Hoxton gent: 'Our street corner won't seem the same without ol' 'arry leaning on the lamp-post keeping an eye out for the coppers.'

Newspapers have become the place to announce weddings, and just occasionally they were able to report on some unexpected outcomes. This short piece comes from the Hackney Mercury *of 4 August 1885.*

EXTRAORDINARY SCENE AT HACKNEY

When a man goes a wooing, he does not, as a rule, turn the worst side of his affairs out for the inspection of his lady-love and her family. Rather on the contrary, he is apt to throw a little couleur-de-rose over his prospects, and state his position in a manner that makes the connubial state much to be envied. This evidently was the case with the individual who, last Saturday evening, lost possession of his 'better-half' in the Graham-road, Hackney. They had that morning secretly tied the nuptial knot and were proceeding to their abode at South Hackney, where a furnished apartment at a moderate rental and a pleasant landlady awaited them. They were especially noticeable to the passing passengers by their light wedding attire and the abundance of seasonable flowers which bedecked them; and being thus engaged in earnest conversation, did not observe the near approach of the mother of the bride, who had

Graham Road, *c.* 1910.

been closely watching their movements. From some independent source the irate mother-in-law had heard of the secret marriage, and the fact that 'George' and the coin of the realm were perfect strangers, and had determined to watch them to their new home. But her passion overcame her, and when near the railway arch in the Graham-road, she pounced upon the happy couple, and striking the newly polished hat of the bridegroom with her umbrella, declared that her 'beloved daughter' should never live with him. This assault was closely followed by the contents of a small bag of flour, which, being thrown with considerable force, almost blinded the astonished husband, and made the situation extremely ridiculous. At this juncture a hansom cab came rolling up the road, and before the bridegroom had recovered sufficiently to realize his position, his wife and her mother had disappeared.

Local papers provided columns for women from the 1890s with pieces on household management, food and clothes, but comments on fashion appeared much earlier. In 1950 the Hackney Gazette *reprinted a letter from the paper of 2 April 1870, from 'An English Hackney Girl':*

For some time I have noticed the growing evil of fast dressing in our sisters of England. Until within the last few years they have been noted for their simplicity and retiring qualities. Now they surpass our neighbours, the French girls, in dress forwardness, and in fact all that is unwomanly. 'The Grecian Bend' and 'The Princess Limp' are the latest follies and I am truly sorry to see now many silly girls, even in our quiet neighbourhood of Hackney, following these ridiculous fashions.

'Girls', she enjoined 'if you want a husband, don't go limping along the streets as if you had one leg shorter than the other, nor bend forwards as if you were afraid of looking anyone straight in the face. I know if I were a man, I should not choose my partner for life from either the Grecian Benders or the Princess Limpers.'

The following piece of advice for the aspiring well-dressed north-London woman comes from the pages of the Stoke Newington Observer *on 12 April 1940.*

MEN, WOMEN AND CLOTHES
Chenille
Chenille is big fashion news this season. Chenille pompoms decorate gay spring hats. Little evening bags are crocheted in black or red chenille. Elbow length gloves have tiny tassels of soft chenille round the edge of the gauntlet and brightly coloured chenille scarves are worn with town or country suit. An evening bag of grey chenille crochet, lined with lavender silk, has an old fashioned gold clasp inset with round-cut garnets. A hair snood of scarlet and green chenille is fastened with a thick jade brooch. . . .

'Economical undies – petti-knicks', from the pages of the *Stoke Newington Observer*, 26 April 1940.

119

Summer Suits

The news that the Army is going into cotton battle dress for the summer will jerk the minds of many civilians who have so far not thought out their summer suit. While respecting the old saying 'ne'er cast a clout til May be out', many men of restricted means start putting by the odd fifty shillings or so for their summer suit while April showers are still warning them to carry an umbrella. Few men will follow the example of the Army far enough to buy themselves a cotton suit, but according to the tailors, light-weight wool materials in gay check patterns are likely to be much in demand.

That 1940 Look

A touch of white enlivens up an old suit or frock and gives last year's model that 1940 look. White pique collars and cuffs – detachable; of course – or white wool stitched on a dark coloured suit are two good renovating ideas. A white chiffon scarf, boldly embroidered with initials to match gloves or handbag, can be worn with high necked dresses or as a sash round the waist. A necklace and clip-on earrings of carved ivory or a big cameo brooch of white onyx are effective pieces of white jewellery to brighten a sober suit.

And for that final patriotic touch tricolour dresses or red, white and blue ribbons should brighten up your war. . . .

The Hackney Gazette *expanded its women's material to a whole page with recipes, fashion, relevant news and features. One piece that appeared on 13 February 1970 on the experiences of a former local woman, the wife of an Edgware kosher butcher, with losing weight, as related to the Hackney branch of Weight Watchers, clearly gave one sub the chance he had been waiting for and he headed the piece 'Pearl Schlagman is no longer a "fatty"'.*

In December 1953, Hackney was still receiving food parcels from the USA as presents for old people, but the decade was to see the beginning of an explosion of youth culture. Stars visited Hackney and were duly mobbed – contemporary local journalese speak for a very warm reception. Singer and film star Petula Clark was at Dalston, as reported in one local paper for 4 April 1952, when she performed at the Dalston Odeon, afterwards signing autographs and posing for pictures in the foyer in a pink tulle dress embroidered with sequins. But by 1955 it was the real thing. This report came from the Hackney Gazette *of 3 October:*

HACKNEY'S MAD SATURDAY. ALL THROUGH JOHNNIE RAY VISIT TO YOUTH CLUB
Girls screamed, tore their hair and jumped up and down hysterically. Police fought to hold them back as, for 10 minutes, a tall young man in a tweed jacket tried to force his way out of a big black car. . . . Not an American scene this – it happened on Saturday in Hackney. Johnnie Ray had come to town.

He had come to see for himself the Springfield Boys' Club, Clapton . . . the club whose patron he agreed to be many months ago. Clapton turned out in full force to see for themselves this fabulous American 'Cry' singer.

Inside the club, after he had fought his way in with his coat ripped off, Johnnie posed for pictures and told a Gazette reporter: 'I have always been interested in youth clubs. I chose this boys club because . . . well . . . every boy needs a big brother. The girls? They can certainly stand up for themselves.' Outside the girls howled. 'Do I think that hysteria is any good for them?' echoed Mr Ray. 'It can't be any more than shouting your lungs out at a football match.'

The club premises were packed to capacity as Johnnie made an inspection. In the street crowds of teenage girls fought for positions near windows. Excitement grew as Johnnie, surrounded by club members and girls, invited all to sing with him 'Walkie my Baby Back Home'. . . .

Rooms seemed to bulge as the singer's fans packed in to

'It's here – the Twist!' – in progress at a St Leonard's Hospital dance, January 1962.

be near him. A game of billiards with Johnnie must have seemed like playing with little atom bombs to the Mayor (also in attendance). And when Johnnie went to play darts with some of the boys it was like a movie set with ITA cameras rolling and flashlight bulbs popping.

An hour and a half later Johnnie made his way to the door, waved to the people inside the club, took a deep breath and went out. . . .

He made his escape over an adjoining shed roof, with a pack of girls in jeans in hot pursuit. Club officials collaborated with police to hold back the crowd as Mr Ray leaped down from the roof and raced for his car. Back on the roof a girl beat herself on the head and shouted hysterically for Johnnie to 'Come back'.

'Jayne among the birds'. Film star Jayne Mansfield visited the East London Budgerigar and Foreign Birds Society's show at All Saints' Church Hall, Haggerston, in September 1959. Fans were out in force to give her 'a rapturous reception'.

In the 1960s the Hackney Gazette *added a 'Spotlight on Youth' page to the paper. On 2 January 1970 the spotlight was turned back to the decade that had just passed, in a piece composed from four interviews, curiously all with men:*

Nineteen-years-old Alan Fields of Stamford Hill, with shoulder length blond hair, trench coat down to his ankles and a wispy beard, said 'Society has got rid of a lot of hang ups in the Sixties. There is not so much of a taboo on the human body any more. Young people express themselves more freely now and don't care what the older generation thinks about them. I think that it's a good thing that people are throwing off their inhibitions because doing just what you want keeps you happy. For me the most important thing to happen in the Sixties is the appearance of groups like the Beatles and the Stones.'

Peter Cartman, 20, with longish dark hair and a three piece suit, thought that 'the whole youth scene in the Sixties – especially drugs – was a bit sick. If these teenagers were striving for peace how come they were associated with violence? From the teddy boys, mods and rockers up to today's lot.'

For him, the moon landing was the most important event. Colin Brown, 18, choose the England victory in the 1966 football world cup, while Michael Patterson, focused on the horror of the wars in Vietnam and Biafra.

If it wasn't one thing, it was another. On 3 July 1981, the Hackney Gazette *reported on Hackney Council's concern with the latest youth menace, Space Invaders, when they attempted to limit the number of video games any café or shop could have to three. Hopeful of new revenue, the then borough solicitor even suggested locally taxing them, though this would have required national legislation. But in an earlier era they made their own entertainments. This extract from a much longer piece comes from the* Hackney Gazette *in 1911.*

Stoke Newington Common, *c.* 1905.

DEVON BULLOCK RUNS AMOK IN STOKE NEWINGTON

Awaiting sentence of death in a stall contiguous to Mr R. Row's slaughter-house in Brooke-road, a Devon bullock availed itself of the opportunity of slipping out of the door, which had been momentarily left unfastened. The animal, having got into the shop, found the glass door shut; but it surmounted this obstacle by plunging through it and smashing it to smithereens. The bullock's pachydermatous hide was unscathed and it scampered up High-street towards Stamford hill. Attempts were made to drive the fugitive back, but this only accelerated its speed. On reaching Garnham-street, it may be that its eye caught sight of the Jolly Butchers public house. This naturally caused it to stop, as if between the devil and the deep sea. But realising that to halt would be fatal, it rushed down Garnham-street, whence it took to Stoke Newington common. By this time its butcher enemies were on its track, but when they had induced it to the slaughterhouse door it refused to enter – its unwillingness is ascribed to the crowd of children who had followed it and hampered it from going in. Back it rushed to the Common, and kept its pursuers at bay for nearly an hour. Stoke Newington common was like a bull ring, and the policemen had their work cut out to keep the people, especially the children, out of the danger zone, although the bullock did not manifest any symptoms of bovine ferocity. . . .

INDEX

Because of considerations of space, only people who appear in pictures have been included in the index, which otherwise covers subjects and places. *Italics* indicate a picture as well as text.